The Meaning of
TRUTH

William James

DOVER PUBLICATIONS, INC.
Mineola, New York

Published in Canada by General Publishing Company, Ltd., 895
Don Mills Road, 400-2 Park Centre, Toronto, Ontario M3C 1W3.
Published in the United Kingdom by David & Charles, Brunel
House, Forde Close, Newton Abbot, Devon TQ12 4PU.

Bibliographical Note

This Dover edition, first published in 2002, is an unabridged
republication of the 1932 printing of the 1909 edition of the work
originally published by Longmans, Green, and Co., New York and
London.

Library of Congress Cataloging-in-Publication Data

James, William, 1842-1910.
    The meaning of truth / William James.
        p. cm.
    Originally published: New York : Longmans, Green, 1909.
    ISBN 0-486-42140-6 (pbk.)
    1. Truth. 2. Pragmatism. I. Title.

B945.J23 M27 2002
144'.3—dc21

                                                    2002019434

Manufactured in the United States of America
Dover Publications, Inc., 31 East 2nd Street, Mineola, N.Y. 11501

PREFACE

THE pivotal part of my book named *Pragmatism* is its account of the relation called 'truth' which may obtain between an idea (opinion, belief, statement, or what not) and its object. 'Truth,' I there say, 'is a property of certain of our ideas. It means their agreement, as falsity means their disagreement, with reality. Pragmatists and intellectualists both accept this definition as a matter of course.

'Where our ideas [do] not copy definitely their object, what does agreement with that object mean? . . . Pragmatism asks its usual question. "Grant an idea or belief to be true," it says, "what concrete difference will its being true make in any one's actual life? What experiences [may] be different from those which would obtain if the belief were false? How will the truth be realized? What, in short, is the truth's cash-value in experiential terms?" The moment pragmatism asks this question, it sees the answer: *True ideas are those that we*

can assimilate, validate, corroborate, and verify.
False ideas are those that we cannot. That is
the practical difference it makes to us to have
true ideas; that therefore is the meaning of
truth, for it is all that truth is known as.

'The truth of an idea is not a stagnant property inherent in it. Truth *happens* to an idea.
It *becomes* true, is *made* true by events. Its
verity *is* in fact an event, a process, the process
namely of its verifying itself, its *verification.*
Its validity is the process of its valid*ation.*[1]

'To agree in the widest sense with a reality
can only mean to be guided either straight up
to it or into its surroundings, or to be put into
such working touch with it as to handle either
it or something connected with it better than if
we disagreed. Better either intellectually or
practically. . . . Any idea that helps us to

[1] But '*verifiability,*' I add, 'is as good as verification. For
one truth-process completed, there are a million in our lives
that function in [the] state of nascency. They lead us towards
direct verification; lead us into the surroundings of the object
they envisage; and then, if everything runs on harmoniously,
we are so sure that verification is possible that we omit it,
and are usually justified by all that happens.'

deal, whether practically or intellectually, with
either the reality or its belongings, that does n't
entangle our progress in frustrations, that *fits*,
in fact, and adapts our life to the reality's
whole setting, will agree sufficiently to meet the
requirement. It will be true of that reality.

'*The true*, to put it very briefly, *is only the
expedient in the way of our thinking, just as
the right is only the expedient in the way of our
behaving.* Expedient in almost any fashion,
and expedient in the long run and on the whole,
of course; for what meets expediently all the
experience in sight won't necessarily meet all
farther experiences equally satisfactorily. Experience, as we know, has ways of *boiling over*,
and making us correct our present formulas.'

This account of truth, following upon the
similar ones given by Messrs. Dewey and
Schiller, has occasioned the liveliest discussion.
Few critics have defended it, most of them have
scouted it. It seems evident that the subject is
a hard one to understand, under its apparent
simplicity; and evident also, I think, that the
definitive settlement of it will mark a turning-

point in the history of epistemology, and consequently in that of general philosophy. In order to make my own thought more accessible to those who hereafter may have to study the question, I have collected in the volume that follows all the work of my pen that bears directly on the truth-question. My first statement was in 1884, in the article that begins the present volume. The other papers follow in the order of their publication. Two or three appear now for the first time.

One of the accusations which I oftenest have had to meet is that of making the truth of our religious beliefs consist in their 'feeling good' to us, and in nothing else. I regret to have given some excuse for this charge, by the unguarded language in which, in the book *Pragmatism*, I spoke of the truth of the belief of certain philosophers in the absolute. Explaining why I do not believe in the absolute myself (p. 78), yet finding that it may secure 'moral holidays' to those who need them, and is true in so far forth (if to gain moral holidays be a good),[1] I offered

---

[1] *Op. cit.*, p. 75.

this as a conciliatory olive-branch to my enemies. But they, as is only too common with
such offerings, trampled the gift under foot and
turned and rent the giver. I had counted too
much on their good will — oh for the rarity of
christian charity under the sun! Oh for the
rarity of ordinary secular intelligence also! I
had supposed it to be matter of common obser-
vation that, of two competing views of the universe which in all other respects are equal, but
of which the first denies some vital human need
while the second satisfies it, the second will be
favored by sane men for the simple reason that
it makes the world seem more rational. To
choose the first view under such circumstances
would be an ascetic act, an act of philosophic
self-denial of which no normal human being
would be guilty. Using the pragmatic test of the
meaning of concepts, I had shown the concept
of the absolute to *mean* nothing but the holiday
giver, the banisher of cosmic fear. One's objective deliverance, when one says 'the absolute exists,' amounted, on my showing, just to
this, that 'some justification of a feeling of se-

curity in presence of the universe,' exists, and
that systematically to refuse to cultivate a feeling of security would be to do violence to a
tendency in one's emotional life which might
well be respected as prophetic.

Apparently my absolutist critics fail to see
the workings of their own minds in any such
picture, so all that I can do is to apologize, and
take my offering back. The absolute is true in
no way then, and least of all, by the verdict of
the critics, in the way which I assigned!

My treatment of 'God,' 'freedom,' and 'de-
sign' was similar. Reducing, by the pragmatic
test, the meaning of each of these concepts to
its positive experienceable operation, I showed
them all to mean the same thing, viz., the presence of 'promise' in the world. 'God or no
God?' means 'promise or no promise?' It
seems to me that the alternative is objective
enough, being a question as to whether the
cosmos has one character or another, even
though our own provisional answer be made on
subjective grounds. Nevertheless christian and
non-christian critics alike accuse me of sum-

moning people to say 'God exists,' *even when he does n't exist*, because forsooth in my philosophy the 'truth' of the saying does n't really mean that he exists in any shape whatever, but only that to say so feels good.

Most of the pragmatist and anti-pragmatist warfare is over what the word 'truth' shall be held to signify, and not over any of the facts embodied in truth-situations; for both pragmatists and anti-pragmatists believe in existent objects, just as they believe in our ideas of them. The difference is that when the pragmatists speak of truth, they mean exclusively something about the ideas, namely their workableness; whereas when anti-pragmatists speak of truth they seem most often to mean something about the objects. Since the pragmatist, if he agrees that an idea is 'really' true, also agrees to whatever it says about its object; and since most anti-pragmatists have already come round to agreeing that, if the object exists, the idea that it does so is workable; there would seem so little left to fight about that I might well be asked why instead of reprinting my share in so much verbal wrangling, I do not show my sense of 'values' by burning it all up.

I understand the question and I will give my answer. I am interested in another doctrine in philosophy to which I give the name of radical empiricism, and it seems to me that the establishment of the pragmatist theory of truth is a step of first-rate importance in making radical empiricism prevail. Radical empiricism consists first of a postulate, next of a statement of fact, and finally of a generalized conclusion.

The postulate is that the only things that shall be debatable among philosophers shall be things definable in terms drawn from experience. [Things of an unexperienceable nature may exist ad libitum, but they form no part of the material for philosophic debate.]

The statement of fact is that the relations between things, conjunctive as well as disjunctive, are just as much matters of direct particular experience, neither more so nor less so, than the things themselves.

The generalized conclusion is that therefore

the parts of experience hold together from next
to next by relations that are themselves parts of
experience. The directly apprehended universe
needs, in short, no extraneous trans-empirical
connective support, but possesses in its own
right a concatenated or continuous structure.

The great obstacle to radical empiricism in
the contemporary mind is the rooted rationalist
belief that experience as immediately given is
all disjunction and no conjunction, and that
to make one world out of this separateness,
a higher unifying agency must be there. In
the prevalent idealism this agency is represented as the absolute all-witness which 'relates' things together by throwing 'categories'
over them like a net. The most peculiar and
unique, perhaps, of all these categories is supposed to be the truth-relation, which connects
parts of reality in pairs, making of one of them
a knower, and of the other a thing known,
yet which is itself contentless experientially,
neither describable, explicable, nor reduceable
to lower terms, and denotable only by uttering
the name 'truth.'

The pragmatist view, on the contrary, of the truth-relation is that it has a definite content, and that everything in it is experienceable. Its whole nature can be told in positive terms. The 'workableness' which ideas must have, in order to be true, means particular workings, physical or intellectual, actual or possible, which they may set up from next to next inside of concrete experience. Were this pragmatic contention admitted, one great point in the victory of radical empiricism would also be scored, for the relation between an object and the idea that truly knows it, is held by rationalists to be nothing of this describable sort, but to stand outside of all possible temporal experience; and on the relation, so interpreted, rationalism is wonted to make its last most obdurate rally.

Now the anti-pragmatist contentions which I try to meet in this volume can be so easily used by rationalists as weapons of resistance, not only to pragmatism but to radical empiricism also (for if the truth-relation were transcendent, others might be so too), that I feel strongly

the strategical importance of having them
definitely met and got out of the way. What
our critics most persistently keep saying is that
though workings go with truth, yet they do not
constitute it. It is numerically additional to
them, prior to them, explanatory *of* them, and
in no wise to be explained *by* them, we are
incessantly told. The first point for our enemies to establish, therefore, is that *something*
numerically additional and prior to the workings is involved in the truth of an idea. Since
the *object* is additional, and usually prior, most
rationalists plead *it*, and boldly accuse us of
denying it. This leaves on the bystanders the
impression — since we cannot reasonably deny
the existence of the object — that our account
of truth breaks down, and that our critics have
driven us from the field. Altho in various places
in this volume I try to refute the slanderous
charge that we deny real existence, I will say
here again, for the sake of emphasis, that the
existence of the object, whenever the idea asserts it 'truly,' is the only reason, in innumerable cases, why the idea does work successfully,

if it work at all; and that it seems an abuse of language, to say the least, to transfer the word 'truth' from the idea to the object's existence, when the falsehood of ideas that won't work is explained by that existence as well as the truth of those that will.

I find this abuse prevailing among my most accomplished adversaries. But once establish the proper verbal custom, let the word 'truth' represent a property of the idea, cease to make it something mysteriously connected with the object known, and the path opens fair and wide, as I believe, to the discussion of radical empiricism on its merits. The truth of an idea will then mean only its workings, or that in it which by ordinary psychological laws sets up those workings; it will mean neither the idea's object, nor anything 'saltatory' inside the idea, that terms drawn from experience cannot describe.

One word more, ere I end this preface. A distinction is sometimes made between Dewey, Schiller and myself, as if I, in supposing the object's existence, made a concession to popu-

lar prejudice which they, as more radical pragmatists, refuse to make. As I myself understand these authors, we all three absolutely agree
in admitting the transcendency of the object
(provided it be an experienceable object) to the
subject, in the truth-relation. Dewey in particular has insisted almost ad nauseam that the
whole meaning of our cognitive states and processes lies in the way they intervene in the control and revaluation of independent existences
or facts. His account of knowledge is not only
absurd, but meaningless, unless independent
existences be there of which our ideas take
account, and for the transformation of which
they work. But because he and Schiller refuse
to discuss objects and relations 'transcendent'
in the sense of being *altogether trans-experiential*, their critics pounce on sentences in their
writings to that effect to show that they deny
the existence *within the realm of experience*
of objects external to the ideas that declare
their presence there.[1] It seems incredible

---

[1] It gives me pleasure to welcome Professor Carveth Read
into the pragmatistic church, so far as his epistemology

that educated and apparently sincere critics should so fail to catch their adversary's point of view.

What misleads so many of them is possibly also the fact that the universes of discourse of Schiller, Dewey, and myself are panoramas of different extent, and that what the one postulates explicitly the other provisionally leaves only in a state of implication, while the reader thereupon considers it to be denied. Schiller's universe is the smallest, being essentially a psychological one. He starts with but one sort of thing, truth-claims, but is led ultimately to the independent objective facts which they

goes. See his vigorous book, *The Metaphysics of Nature*, 2d Edition, Appendix A. (London, Black, 1908.) The work *What is Reality?* by Francis Howe Johnson (Boston, 1891), of which I make the acquaintance only while correcting these proofs, contains some striking anticipations of the later pragmatist view. *The Psychology of Thinking*, by Irving E. Miller (New York, Macmillan Co., 1909), which has just appeared, is one of the most convincing pragmatist documents yet published, tho it does not use the word 'pragmatism' at all. While I am making references, I cannot refrain from inserting one to the extraordinarily acute article by H. V. Knox, in the *Quarterly Review* for April, 1909.

assert, inasmuch as the most successfully vali-
dated of all claims is that such facts are there.
My universe is more essentially epistemological. I start with two things, the objective facts
and the claims, and indicate which claims, the
facts being there, will work successfully as the
latter's substitutes and which will not. I call
the former claims true. Dewey's panorama, if
I understand this colleague, is the widest of the
three, but I refrain from giving my own account
of its complexity. Suffice it that he holds as
firmly as I do to objects independent of our
judgments. If I am wrong in saying this, he
must correct me. I decline in this matter to be
corrected at second hand.

I have not pretended in the following pages
to consider all the critics of my account of
truth, such as Messrs. Taylor, Lovejoy, Gardi-
ner, Bakewell, Creighton, Hibben, Parodi,
Salter, Carus, Lalande, Mentré, McTaggart,
G. E. Moore, Ladd and others, especially
not Professor Schinz, who has published under
the title of *Anti-pragmatisme* an amusing
sociological romance. Some of these critics

PREFACE

seem to me to labor under an inability almost pathetic, to understand the thesis which they seek to refute. I imagine that most of their difficulties have been answered by anticipation elsewhere in this volume, and I am sure that my readers will thank me for not adding more repetition to the fearful amount that is already there.

95 Irving St., Cambridge (Mass.),
August, 1909.

CONTENTS

xxi

CONTENTS

I

THE FUNCTION OF COGNITION[1]

THE following inquiry is (to use a distinction familiar to readers of Mr. Shadworth Hodgson) not an inquiry into the 'how it comes,' but into the 'what it is' of cognition. What we call acts of cognition are evidently realized through what we call brains and their events, whether there be 'souls' dynamically connected with the brains or not. But with neither brains nor souls has this essay any business to transact. In it we shall simply assume that cognition *is* produced, somehow, and limit ourselves to asking what elements it contains, what factors it implies.

Cognition is a function of consciousness. The first factor it implies is therefore a state of consciousness wherein the cognition shall take place. Having elsewhere used the word 'feel-

[1] Read before the Aristotelian Society, December 1, 1884, and first published in *Mind*, vol. x (1885). — This, and the following articles have received a very slight verbal revision, consisting mostly in the omission of redundancy.

ing' to designate generically all states of consciousness considered subjectively, or without respect to their possible function, I shall then say that, whatever elements an act of cognition may imply besides, it at least implies the existence of a *feeling*. [If the reader share the current antipathy to the word 'feeling,' he may substitute for it, wherever I use it, the word 'idea,' taken in the old broad Lockian sense, or he may use the clumsy phrase 'state of consciousness,' or finally he may say 'thought' instead.]

Now it is to be observed that the common consent of mankind has agreed that some feelings are cognitive and some are simple facts having a subjective, or, what one might almost call a physical, existence, but no such self-transcendent function as would be implied in their being pieces of knowledge. Our task is again limited here. We are not to ask, 'How is self-transcendence possible?' We are only to ask, 'How comes it that common sense has assigned a number of cases in which it is assumed not only to be possible but actual? And what are the marks used by common sense to

2

distinguish those cases from the rest?' In short, our inquiry is a chapter in descriptive psychology, — hardly anything more.

Condillac embarked on a quest similar to this by his famous hypothesis of a statue to which various feelings were successively imparted. Its first feeling was supposed to be one of fragrance. But to avoid all possible complication with the question of genesis, let us not attribute even to a statue the possession of our imaginary feeling. Let us rather suppose it attached to no matter, nor localized at any point in space, but left swinging *in vacuo*, as it were, by the direct creative *fiat* of a god. And let us also, to escape entanglement with difficulties about the physical or psychical nature of its 'object,' not call it a feeling of fragrance or of any other determinate sort, but limit ourselves to assuming that it is a feeling of *q*. What is true of it under this abstract name will be no less true of it in any more particular shape (such as fragrance, pain, hardness) which the reader may suppose.

Now, if this feeling of *q* be the only creation

of the god, it will of course form the entire universe. And if, to escape the cavils of that large class of persons who believe that *semper idem sentire ac non sentire* are the same,[1] we allow the feeling to be of as short a duration as they like, that universe will only need to last an infinitesimal part of a second. The feeling in question will thus be reduced to its fighting weight, and all that befalls it in the way of a cognitive function must be held to befall in the brief instant of its quickly snuffed-out life, — a life, it will also be noticed, that has no other moment

---

[1] 'The Relativity of Knowledge,' held in this sense, is, it may be observed in passing, one of the oddest of philosophic superstitions. Whatever facts may be cited in its favor are due to the properties of nerve-tissue, which may be exhausted by too prolonged an excitement. Patients with neuralgias that last unremittingly for days can, however, assure us that the limits of this nerve-law are pretty widely drawn. But if we physically could get a feeling that should last eternally unchanged, what atom of logical or psychological argument is there to prove that it would not be felt as long as it lasted, and felt for just what it is, all that time? The reason for the opposite prejudice seems to be our reluctance to think that so *stupid* a thing as such a feeling would necessarily be, should be allowed to fill eternity with its presence. An interminable acquaintance, leading to no knowledge-*about*, — such would ,be its condition.

of consciousness either preceding or following it.

Well now, can our little feeling, thus left alone in the universe, — for the god and we psychological critics may be supposed left out of the account, — can the feeling, I say, be said to have any sort of a cognitive function? For it to *know*, there must be something to be known. What is there, on the present supposition? One may reply, 'the feeling's content q.' But does it not seem more proper to call this the feeling's *quality* than its content? Does not the word 'content' suggest that the feeling has already dirempted itself as an act from its content as an object? And would it be quite safe to assume so promptly that the quality q of a feeling is one and the same thing with a feeling of the quality q? The quality q, so far, is an entirely subjective fact which the feeling carries so to speak endogenously, or in its pocket. If any one pleases to dignify so simple a fact as this by the name of knowledge, of course nothing can prevent him. But let us keep closer to the path of common usage, and reserve the name knowledge for the cognition of 'realities,' meaning by realities things that exist independently of the feeling through which their cognition occurs. If the content of the feeling occur nowhere in the universe outside of the feeling itself, and perish with the feeling, common usage refuses to call it a reality, and brands it as a subjective feature of the feeling's constitution, or at the most as the feeling's *dream*.

For the feeling to be cognitive in the specific sense, then, it must be self-transcendent; and we must prevail upon the god to *create a reality outside of it* to correspond to its intrinsic quality q. Thus only can it be redeemed from the condition of being a solipsism. If now the new-created reality *resemble* the feeling's quality q, I say that the feeling may be held by us *to be cognizant of that reality*.

This first instalment of my thesis is sure to be attacked. But one word before defending it. 'Reality' has become our warrant for calling a feeling cognitive; but what becomes our warrant for calling anything reality? The only reply is — the faith of the present critic or in-quirer. At every moment of his life he finds himself subject to a belief in *some* realities, even though his realities of this year should prove to be his illusions of the next. Whenever he finds that the feeling he is studying contemplates what he himself regards as a reality, he must of course admit the feeling itself to be truly cognitive. We are ourselves the critics here; and we shall find our burden much lightened by being allowed to take reality in this relative and provisional way. Every science must make some assumptions. *Erkenntnisstheoretiker* are but fallible mortals. When they study the function of cognition, they do it by means of the same function in themselves. And knowing that the fountain cannot go higher than its source, we should promptly confess that our results in this field are affected by our own lia-bility to err. *The most we can claim is, that what we say about cognition may be counted as true as what we say about anything else.* If our hearers agree with us about what are to be held 'realities,' they will perhaps also agree to the reality of our doctrine of the way in which they are known. We cannot ask for more.

Our terminology shall follow the spirit of these remarks. We will deny the function of knowledge to any feeling whose quality or content we do not ourselves believe to exist outside of that feeling as well as in it. We may call such a feeling a dream if we like; we shall have to see later whether we can call it a fiction or an error.

To revert now to our thesis. Some persons will immediately cry out, 'How *can* a reality resemble a feeling?' Here we find how wise we were to name the quality of the feeling by an algebraic letter q. We flank the whole difficulty of resemblance between an inner state and an outward reality, by leaving it free to any one to postulate as the reality whatever sort of thing he thinks *can* resemble a feeling, — if not an outward thing, then another feeling like the first one, — the mere feeling q in the critic's mind for example. Evading thus this objection, we turn to another which is sure to be urged.

It will come from those philosophers to whom 'thought,' in the sense of a knowledge of relations, is the all in all of mental life; and who hold a merely feeling consciousness to be no better — one would sometimes say from their utterances, a good deal worse — than no consciousness at all. Such phrases as these, for example, are common to-day in the mouths of those who claim to walk in the footprints of Kant and Hegel rather than in the ancestral English paths : 'A perception detached from all others, "left out of the heap we call a mind," being out of all relation, has no qualities — is simply nothing. We can no more consider it than we can see vacancy.' 'It is simply in itself fleeting, momentary, unnameable (because while we name it it has become another), and for the very same reason unknowable, the very negation of knowability.' 'Exclude from what we have considered real all qualities constituted by relation, we find that none are left.'

Altho such citations as these from the writings of Professor Green might be multiplied almost indefinitely, they would hardly repay the pains of collection, so egregiously false is the doctrine they teach. Our little supposed feeling, whatever it may be, from the cognitive point of view, whether a bit of knowledge or a dream, is certainly no psychical zero. It is a most positively and definitely qualified inner fact, with a complexion all its own. Of course there are many mental facts which it is *not*. It knows q, if q be a reality, with a very minimum of knowledge. It neither dates nor locates it. It neither classes nor names it. And it neither knows itself as a feeling, nor contrasts itself with other feelings, nor estimates its own duration or intensity. It is, in short, if there is no more of it than this, a most dumb and helpless and useless kind of thing.

But if we must describe it by so many negations, and if it can say nothing *about* itself or *about* anything else, by what right do we deny that it is a psychical zero? And may not the 'relationists' be right after all?

In the innocent looking word 'about' lies the solution of this riddle; and a simple enough solution it is when frankly looked at. A quotation from a too seldom quoted book, the *Exploratio Philosophica* of John Grote (London, 1865), p. 60, will form the best introduction to it.

'Our knowledge,' writes Grote, 'may be contemplated in either of two ways, or, to use other words, we may speak in a double manner of the "object" of knowledge. That is, we may either use language thus: we *know* a thing, a man, etc.; or we may use it thus: we know such and such things *about* the thing, the man, etc. Language in general, following its true logical instinct, distinguishes between these two applications of the notion of knowledge, the one being γνῶναι, *noscere, kennen, connaître,* the other being εἰδέναι, *scire, wissen, savoir.* In the origin, the former may be considered more what I have called phenomenal — it is the notion of knowledge as *acquaintance* or familiarity with what is known; which notion is perhaps more akin to the phenomenal bodily communication, and is less purely intellectual than the other; it is the kind of knowledge which we have of a thing by the presentation

11

to the senses or the representation of it in picture or type, a *Vorstellung*. The other, which is what we express in judgments or propositions, what is embodied in *Begriffe* or concepts without any necessary imaginative representation, is in its origin the more intellectual notion of knowledge. There is no reason, however, why we should not express our knowledge, whatever its kind, in either manner, provided only we do not confusedly express it, in the same proposition or piece of reasoning, in both.'

Now obviously if our supposed feeling of *q* is (if knowledge at all) only knowledge of the mere acquaintance-type, it is milking a he-goat, as the ancients would have said, to try to extract from it any deliverance *about* anything under the sun, even about itself. And it is as unjust, after our failure, to turn upon it and call it a psychical nothing, as it would be, after our fruitless attack upon the billy-goat, to proclaim the non-lactiferous character of the whole goat-tribe. But the entire industry of the Hegelian school in trying to shove simple sensation out of the pale of philosophic recognition is founded on this false issue. It is always the 'speechlessness' of sensation, its inability to make any 'statement,'[1] that is held to make the very notion of it meaningless, and to justify the student of knowledge in scouting it out of existence. 'Significance,' in the sense of standing as the sign of other mental states, is taken to be the sole function of what mental states we have; and from the perception that our little primitive sensation has as yet no significance in this literal sense, it is an easy step to call it first meaningless, next senseless, then vacuous, and finally to brand it as absurd and inadmissible. But in this universal liquidation, this everlasting slip, slip, slip, of direct acquaintance into knowledge-*about*, until at last nothing is left about which the knowledge can be supposed to obtain, does not all 'significance' depart from the situation? And when our knowledge about things has reached its never so complicated perfection, must there

[1] See, for example, Green's Introduction to Hume's *Treatise of Human Nature*, p. 36.

not needs abide alongside of it and inextricably mixed in with it some acquaintance with *what* things all this knowledge is about?

Now, our supposed little feeling gives a *what;* and if other feelings should succeed which remember the first, its *what* may stand as subject or predicate of some piece of knowledge-about, of some judgment, perceiving relations between it and other *whats* which the other feelings may know. The hitherto dumb *q* will then receive a name and be no longer speechless. But every name, as students of logic know, has its 'denotation'; and the denotation always means some reality or content, relationless *ab extra* or with its internal relations unanalyzed, like the *q* which our primitive sensation is supposed to know. No relation-expressing proposition is possible except on the basis of a preliminary acquaintance with such 'facts,' with such contents, as this. Let the *q* be fragrance, let it be toothache, or let it be a more complex kind of feeling, like that of the full-moon swimming in her blue abyss, it must first come in that simple shape, and be held fast in that first intention, before any knowledge *about* it can be attained. The knowledge *about* it is *it* with a context added. Undo *it*, and what is added cannot be *context*.[1]

Let us say no more then about this objection, but enlarge our thesis, thus: If there be in the universe a q other than the q in the feeling, the latter may have acquaintance with an entity ejective to itself; an acquaintance moreover, which, as mere acquaintance, it would be hard to imagine susceptible either of improvement or increase, being in its way complete; and which would oblige us (so long as we refuse not to call acquaintance knowledge) to say not only that the feeling is cognitive, but that all qualities of feeling, *so long as there is*

[1] If A enters and B exclaims, 'Did n't you see my brother on the stairs?' we all hold that A may answer, 'I saw him, but did n't know he was your brother'; ignorance of brotherhood not abolishing power to see. But those who, on account of the unrelatedness of the first facts with which we become acquainted, deny them to be 'known' to us, ought in consistency to maintain that if A did not perceive the relationship of the man on the stairs to B, it was impossible he should have noticed him at all.

anything outside of them which they resemble,
are feelings *of* qualities of existence, and perceptions of outward fact.

The point of this vindication of the cognitive function of the first feeling lies, it will be
noticed, in the discovery that q does exist elsewhere than in it. In case this discovery were
not made, we could not be sure the feeling was
cognitive; and in case there were nothing outside to be discovered, we should have to call
the feeling a dream. But the feeling itself
cannot make the discovery. Its own q is the
only q it grasps; and its own nature is not a
particle altered by having the self-transcendent function of cognition either added to it
or taken away. The function is accidental;
synthetic, not analytic; and falls outside and
not inside its being.[1]

---

[1] It seems odd to call so important a function accidental,
but I do not see how we can mend the matter. Just as, if we
start with the reality and ask how it may come to be known,
we can only reply by invoking a feeling which shall *reconstruct*
it in its own more private fashion; so, if we start with the feeling and ask how it may come to know, we can only reply by
invoking a reality which shall *reconstruct* it in its own more
public fashion. In either case, however, the datum we start

A feeling feels as a gun shoots. If there be nothing to be felt or hit, they discharge themselves *ins blaue hinein.* If, however, something starts up opposite them, they no longer simply shoot or feel, they hit and know.

But with this arises a worse objection than any yet made. We the critics look on and see a real q and a feeling of q; and because the two resemble each other, we say the one knows the other. But what right have we to say this until we know that the feeling of q means to stand for or represent just that *same* other q? Suppose, instead of one q, a number of real q's in the field. If the gun shoots and hits, we can easily see which one of them it hits. But how can we distinguish which one the feeling

with remains just what it was. One may easily get lost in verbal mysteries about the difference between quality of feeling and feeling of quality, between receiving and reconstructing the knowledge of a reality. But at the end we must confess that the notion of real cognition involves an unmediated dualism of the knower and the known. See Bowne's *Metaphysics*, New York, 1882, pp. 403–412, and various passages in Lotze, *e. g., Logic*, § 308. ['Unmediated' is a bad word to have used. — 1909.]

knows? It knows the one it stands for. But which one *does* it stand for? It declares no intention in this respect. It merely resembles; it resembles all indifferently; and resembling, *per se*, is not necessarily representing or standing-for at all. Eggs resemble each other, but do not on that account represent, stand for, or know each other. And if you say this is because neither of them is a *feeling*, then imagine the world to consist of nothing but toothaches, which *are* feelings, feelings resembling each other exactly, — would they know each other the better for all that?

The case of *q* being a bare quality like that of toothache-pain is quite different from that of its being a concrete individual thing. There is practically no test for deciding whether the feeling of a bare quality means to represent it or not. It can *do* nothing to the quality beyond resembling it, simply because an abstract quality is a thing to which nothing can be done. Being without context or environment or *principium individuationis*, a quiddity with no hæcceity, a platonic idea, even duplicate editions of such a quality (were they possible), would be indiscernible, and no sign could be given, no result altered, whether the feeling meant to stand for this edition or for that, or whether it simply resembled the quality without meaning to stand for it at all.

If now we grant a genuine pluralism of editions to the quality q, by assigning to each a *context* which shall distinguish it from its mates, we may proceed to explain which edition of it the feeling knows, by extending our principle of resemblance to the context too, and saying the feeling knows the particular q whose context it most exactly duplicates. But here again the theoretic doubt recurs: duplication and coincidence, are they knowledge? The gun shows which q it points to and hits, by *breaking* it. Until the feeling can show us which q it points to and knows, by some equally flagrant token, why are we not free to deny that it either points to or knows any one of the *real* q's at all, and to affirm that the word 'resemblance' exhaustively describes its relation to the reality?

Well, as a matter of fact, every actual feeling *does* show us, quite as flagrantly as the gun, which q it points to; and practically in concrete cases the matter is decided by an element we have hitherto left out. Let us pass from abstractions to possible instances, and ask our obliging *deus ex machina* to frame for us a richer world. Let him send me, for example, a dream of the death of a certain man, and let him simultaneously cause the man to die. How would our practical instinct spontaneously decide whether this were a case of cognition of the reality, or only a sort of marvellous coincidence of a resembling reality with my dream? Just such puzzling cases as this are what the 'society for psychical research' is busily collecting and trying to interpret in the most reasonable way.

If my dream were the only one of the kind I ever had in my life, if the context of the death in the dream differed in many particulars from the real death's context, and if my dream led me to no action about the death, unquestionably we should all call it a strange coincidence, and naught besides. But if the death in the dream had a long context, agreeing point for point with every feature that attended the real death; if I were constantly having such dreams, all equally perfect, and if on awaking I had a habit of *acting* immediately as if they were true and so getting 'the start' of my more tardily instructed neighbors, — we should in all probability have to admit that I had some mysterious kind of clairvoyant power, that my dreams in an inscrutable way meant just those realities they figured, and that the word 'coincidence' failed to touch the root of the matter. And whatever doubts any one preserved would completely vanish, if it should appear that from the midst of my dream I had the power of *interfering* with the course of the reality, and making the events in it turn this way or that, according as I dreamed they should. Then at least it would be certain that my waking critics and my dreaming self were dealing with the *same*.

And thus do men invariably decide such a question. *The falling of the dream's practical consequences* into the real world, and the *extent*

of the resemblance between the two worlds
are the criteria they instinctively use.[1] All
feeling is for the sake of action, all feeling results in action, — to-day no argument is needed

[1] The thoroughgoing objector might, it is true, still return
to the charge, and, granting a dream which should completely
mirror the real universe, and all the actions dreamed in which
should be instantly matched by duplicate actions in this universe, still insist that this is nothing more than harmony, and
that it is as far as ever from being made clear whether the
dream-world refers to that other world, all of whose details
it so closely copies. This objection leads deep into metaphysics.
I do not impugn its importance, and justice obliges me to say
that but for the teachings of my colleague, Dr. Josiah Royce,
I should neither have grasped its full force nor made my own
practical and psychological point of view as clear to myself
as it is. On this occasion I prefer to stick steadfastly to that
point of view; but I hope that Dr. Royce's more fundamental
criticism of the function of cognition may ere long see the light.
[I referred in this note to Royce's *Religious aspect of philosophy*, then about to be published. This powerful book main-
tained that the notion of *referring* involved that of an inclusive
mind that shall own both the real q and the mental q, and use
the latter expressly as a representative symbol of the former.
At the time I could not refute this transcendentalist opinion.
Later, largely through the influence of Professor D. S. Miller
(see his essay ' The meaning of truth and error,' in the *Philosophical Review* for 1893, vol. 2 p. 403) I came to see that
any definitely experienceable workings would serve as intermediaries quite as well as the absolute mind's intentions
would.]

to prove these truths. But by a most singular disposition of nature which we may conceive to have been different, *my feelings act upon the realities within my critic's world.* Unless, then, my critic can prove that my feeling does not 'point to' those realities which it acts upon, how can he continue to doubt that he and I are alike cognizant of one and the same real world? If the action is performed in one world, that must be the world the feeling intends; if in another world, *that* is the world the feeling has in mind. If your feeling bear no fruits in my world, I call it utterly detached from my world; I call it a solipsism, and call its world a dream-world. If your toothache do not prompt you to *act* as if I had a toothache, nor even as if I had a separate existence; if you neither say to me, 'I know now how you must suffer!' nor tell me of a remedy, I deny that your feeling, however it may resemble mine, is really cognizant of mine. It gives no *sign* of being cognizant, and such a sign is absolutely necessary to my admission that it is.

Before I can think you to mean my world,

you must affect my world; before I can think you to mean much of it, you must affect much of it; and before I can be sure you mean it *as I do*, you must affect it *just as I should* if I were in your place. Then I, your critic, will gladly believe that we are thinking, not only of the same reality, but that we are thinking it *alike*, and thinking of much of its extent.

Without the practical effects of our neighbor's feelings on our own world, we should never suspect the existence of our neighbor's feelings at all, and of course should never find ourselves playing the critic as we do in this article. The constitution of nature is very peculiar. In the world of each of us are certain objects called human bodies, which move about and act on all the other objects there, and the occasions of their action are in the main what the occasions of our action would be, were they our bodies. They use words and gestures, which, if we used them, would have thoughts behind them, — no mere thoughts *überhaupt*, however, but strictly determinate thoughts. I think you have the notion of fire in general, because I see you act towards this fire in my room just as I act towards it, — poke it and present your person towards it, and so forth. But that binds me to believe that if you feel 'fire' at all, *this* is the fire you feel. As a matter of fact, whenever we constitute ourselves into psychological critics, it is not by dint of discovering which reality a feeling 'resembles' that we find out which reality it means. We become first aware of which one it means, and then we suppose that to be the one it resembles. We see each other looking at the same objects, pointing to them and turning them over in various ways, and thereupon we hope and trust that all of our several feelings resemble the reality and each other. But this is a thing of which we are never theoretically sure. Still, it would practically be a case of *grübelsucht*, if a ruffian were assaulting and drubbing my body, to spend much time in subtle speculation either as to whether his vision of my body resembled mine, or as to whether the body he really *meant* to insult were not some body in his mind's eye, altogether other from my own. The practical point of view brushes such metaphysical cobwebs away. If what he have in mind be not *my* body, why call we it a body at all? His mind is inferred by me as a term, to whose existence we trace the things that happen. The inference is quite void if the term, once inferred, be separated from its connection with the body that made me infer it, and connected with another that is not mine at all. No matter for the metaphysical puzzle of how our two minds, the ruffian's and mine, *can* mean the same body. Men who see each other's bodies sharing the same space, treading the same earth, splashing the same water, making the same air resonant, and pursuing the same game and eating out of the same dish, will never practically believe in a pluralism of solipsistic worlds.

Where, however, the actions of one mind seem to take no effect in the world of the other, the case is different. This is what happens in poetry and fiction. Every one knows *Ivanhoe*, for example; but so long as we stick to the story pure and simple without regard to the facts of its production, few would hesitate to admit that there are as many different Ivanhoes as there are different minds cognizant of the story.[1] The fact that all these Ivanhoes

[1] That is, there is no *real* 'Ivanhoe,' not even the one in Sir Walter Scott's mind as he was writing the story. That one is only the *first* one of the Ivanhoe-solipsisms. It is quite true we can make it the real Ivanhoe if we like, and then say that the other Ivanhoes know it or do not know it, according as they refer to and resemble it or no. This is done by bringing in Sir Walter Scott himself as the author of the real Ivanhoe, and so making a complex object of both. This object, however, is not a story pure and simple. It has dynamic relations with the world common to the experience of all the readers. Sir Walter Scott's Ivanhoe got itself printed in volumes which we all can handle, and to any one of which we can refer to see which of our versions be the true one, *i. e.*, the original one of Scott himself. We can see the manuscript; in short we can get back to the Ivanhoe in Scott's mind by many an avenue and channel of this real world of our experience, — a thing we can by no means do with either the Ivanhoe or the Rebecca, either the Templar or the Isaac of York, of the story taken simply as such, and detached from the conditions of its production. Everywhere, then, we have the same test: can we pass continuously from two objects in two minds to a third object which seems to be in *both* minds, because each mind feels every modification imprinted on it by the other? If so, the first two objects named are derivatives, to say the least, from the same third object, and may be held, if they resemble each other, to refer to one and the same reality.

27

resemble each other does not prove the contrary. But if an alteration invented by one man in his version were to reverberate immediately through all the other versions, and produce changes therein, we should then easily agree that all these thinkers were thinking the *same* Ivanhoe, and that, fiction or no fiction, it formed a little world common to them all.

Having reached this point, we may take up our thesis and improve it again. Still calling the reality by the name of q and letting the critic's feeling vouch for it, we can say that any other feeling will be held cognizant of q, provided it both resemble q, and refer to q, as shown by its either modifying q directly, or modifying some other reality, p or r, which the critic knows to be continuous with q. Or more shortly, thus: *The feeling of q knows whatever reality it resembles, and either directly or indirectly operates on.* If it resemble without operating, it is a dream; if it operate without resembling, it is an error.[1]

---

[1] Among such errors are those cases in which our feeling operates on a reality which it does partially resemble, and yet

THE FUNCTION OF COGNITION

It is to be feared that the reader may consider this formula rather insignificant and obvious, and hardly worth the labor of so many

does not intend: as for instance, when I take up your umbrella, meaning to take my own. I cannot be said here either to know your umbrella, or my own, which latter my feeling more completely resembles. I am mistaking them both, misrepresenting their context, etc.

We have spoken in the text as if the critic were necessarily one mind, and the feeling criticised another. But the criticised feeling and its critic may be earlier and later feelings of the same mind, and here it might seem that we could dispense with the notion of operating, to prove that critic and criticised are referring to and meaning to represent the *same*. We think we see our past feelings directly, and know what they refer to without appeal. At the worst, we can always fix the intention of our present feeling and *make* it refer to the same reality to which any one of our past feelings may have referred. So we need no 'operating' here, to make sure that the feeling and its critic mean the same real q. Well, all the better if this is so! We have covered the more complex and difficult case in our text, and we may let this easier one go. The main thing at present is to stick to practical psychology, and ignore metaphysical difficulties.

One more remark. Our formula contains, it will be observed, nothing to correspond to the great principle of cognition laid down by Professor Ferrier in his *Institutes of Metaphysic* and apparently adopted by all the followers of Fichte, the principle, namely, that for knowledge to be constituted there must be knowledge of the knowing mind along with whatever else is known: not q, as we have supposed, but q

29

pages, especially when he considers that the only cases to which it applies are *percepts*, and that the whole field of symbolic or conceptual thinking seems to elude its grasp. Where the reality is either a material thing or act, or a state of the critic's consciousness, I may both mirror it in my mind and operate upon it — in the latter case indirectly, of course — as soon as I perceive it. But there are many cognitions, universally allowed to be such, which neither mirror nor operate on their realities.

In the whole field of symbolic thought we are universally held both to intend, to speak of, and to reach conclusions about — to know in short — particular realities, without having in our subjective consciousness any mind-stuff that resembles them even in a remote degree.

plus myself, must be the least I can know. It is certain that the common sense of mankind never dreams of using any such principle when it tries to discriminate between conscious states that are knowledge and conscious states that are not. So that Ferrier's principle, if it have any relevancy at all, must have relevancy to the metaphysical possibility of consciousness at large, and not to the practically recognized constitution of cognitive consciousness. We may therefore pass it by without further notice here.

We are instructed about them by language which awakens no consciousness beyond its sound; and we know *which* realities they are by the faintest and most fragmentary glimpse of some remote context they may have and by no direct imagination of themselves. As minds may differ here, let me speak in the first person. I am sure that my own current thinking has *words* for its almost exclusive subjective material, words which are made intelligible by being referred to some reality that lies beyond the horizon of direct consciousness, and of which I am only aware as of a terminal *more* existing in a certain direction, to which the words might lead but do not lead yet. The *subject*, or *topic*, of the words is usually something towards which I mentally seem to pitch them in a backward way, almost as I might jerk my thumb over my shoulder to point at something, without looking round, if I were only entirely sure that it was there. The *up-shot*, or *conclusion*, of the words is something towards which I seem to incline my head forwards, as if giving assent to its existence, tho all my mind's eye catches sight of may be some tatter of an image connected with it, which tatter, however, if only endued with the feeling of familiarity and reality, makes me feel that the whole to which it belongs is rational and real, and fit to be let pass.

Here then is cognitive consciousness on a large scale, and yet what it knows, it hardly resembles in the least degree. The formula last laid down for our thesis must therefore be made more complete. We may now express it thus: *A percept knows whatever reality it directly or indirectly operates on and resembles; a conceptual feeling, or thought knows* [1] *a reality, whenever it actually or potentially terminates in a percept that operates on, or resembles that reality, or is otherwise connected with it or with its context.* The latter percept may be either sensation or sensorial idea; and when I say the thought must *terminate* in such a percept, I mean that it must ultimately be capable of leading up thereto, — by the way of practical

---

[1] Is an incomplete 'thought about' that reality, that reality is its 'topic,' etc.

experience, if the terminal feeling be a sensation; by the way of logical or habitual suggestion, if it be only an image in the mind. Let an illustration make this plainer. I open the first book I take up, and read the first sentence that meets my eye: 'Newton saw the handiwork of God in the heavens as plainly as Paley in the animal kingdom.' I immediately look back and try to analyze the subjective state in which I rapidly apprehended this sentence as I read it. In the first place there was an obvious feeling that the sentence was intelligible and rational and related to the world of realities. There was also a sense of agreement or harmony between 'Newton,' 'Paley,' and 'God.' There was no apparent image connected with the words 'heavens,' or 'handiwork,' or 'God'; they were words merely. With 'animal kingdom' I think there was the faintest consciousness (it may possibly have been an image of the steps) of the Museum of Zoölogy in the town of Cambridge where I write. With 'Paley' there was an equally faint consciousness of a small dark leather book; and with 'Newton' a pretty distinct vision of the right-hand lower corner of a curling periwig. This is all the mind-stuff I can discover in my first consciousness of the meaning of this sentence, and I am afraid that even not all of this would have been present had I come upon the sentence in a genuine reading of the book, and not picked it out for an experiment. And yet my consciousness was truly cognitive. The sentence is 'about realities' which my psychological critic — for we must not forget him — acknowledges to be such, even as he acknowledges my distinct feeling that they *are* realities, and my acquiescence in the general rightness of what I read of them, to be true knowledge on my part.

Now what justifies my critic in being as lenient as this? This singularly inadequate consciousness of mine, made up of symbols that neither resemble nor affect the realities they stand for, — how can he be sure it is cognizant of the very realities he has himself in mind?

He is sure because in countless like cases he has seen such inadequate and symbolic thoughts, by developing themselves, terminate in percepts that practically modified and presumably resembled his own. By 'developing' themselves is meant obeying their tendencies, following up the suggestions nascently present in them, working in the direction in which they seem to point, clearing up the penumbra, making distinct the halo, unravelling the fringe, which is part of their composition, and in the midst of which their more substantive kernel of subjective content seems consciously to lie. Thus I may develop my thought in the Paley direction by procuring the brown leather volume and bringing the passages about the animal kingdom before the critic's eyes. I may satisfy him that the words mean for me just what they mean for him, by showing him *in concreto* the very animals and their arrangements, of which the pages treat. I may get Newton's works and portraits; or if I follow the line of suggestion of the wig, I may smother my critic in seventeenth-century matters pertaining to Newton's environment, to show that the word 'Newton' has the same *locus* and relations in both our minds. Finally I may, by act and word, persuade him that what I mean by God and the heavens and the analogy of the handiworks, is just what he means also.

My demonstration in the last resort is to his *senses*. My thought makes me act on his senses much as he might himself act on them, were he pursuing the consequences of a perception of his own. Practically then *my* thought terminates in *his* realities. He willingly supposes it, therefore, to be *of* them, and inwardly to *resemble* what his own thought would be, were it of the same symbolic sort as mine. And the pivot and fulcrum and support of his mental persuasion, is the sensible operation which my thought leads me, or may lead, to effect — the bringing of Paley's book, of Newton's portrait, etc., before his very eyes.

In the last analysis, then, we believe that we all know and think about and talk about the same world, because *we believe our* PERCEPTS *are possessed by us in common.* And we believe this because the percepts of each one of us seem to be changed in consequence of changes in the percepts of some one else. What I am for you is in the first instance a percept of your own. Unexpectedly, however, I open and show you a book, uttering certain sounds the while. These acts are also your percepts, but they so resemble acts of yours with feelings prompting them, that you cannot doubt I have the feelings too, or that the book is one book felt in both our worlds. That it is felt in the same way, that my feelings of it resemble yours, is something of which we never can be sure, but which we assume as the simplest hypothesis that meets the case. As a matter of fact, we never *are* sure of it, and, as *erkenntnisstheoretiker*, we can only say that of feelings that should *not* resemble each other, both could not know the same thing at the same time in the same way.[1] If each holds to its own percept as the reality, it is bound to say of the other percept, that, though it may *intend* that reality, and prove this by working change upon it,

[1] Though both might terminate in the same thing and be incomplete thoughts 'about' it.

yet, if it do not resemble it, it is all false and wrong.[1]

If this be so of percepts, how much more so of higher modes of thought! Even in the sphere of sensation individuals are probably different enough. Comparative study of the simplest conceptual elements seems to show a wider divergence still. And when it comes to general theories and emotional attitudes towards life, it is indeed time to say with Thackeray, 'My friend, two different universes walk about under your hat and under mine.'

What can save us at all and prevent us from flying asunder into a chaos of mutually repellent solipsisms? Through what can our several minds commune? Through nothing but the mutual resemblance of those of our perceptual feelings which have this power of

[1] The difference between Idealism and Realism is immaterial here. What is said in the text is consistent with either theory. A law by which my percept shall change yours directly is no more mysterious than a law by which it shall first change a physical reality, and then the reality change yours. In either case you and I seem knit into a continuous world, and not to form a pair of solipsisms.

modifying one another, *which are mere dumb knowledges-of-acquaintance*, and which must also resemble their realities or not know them aright at all. In such pieces of knowledge-of-acquaintance all our knowledge-about must end, and carry a sense of this possible termination as part of its content. These percepts, these *termini*, these sensible things, these mere matters-of-acquaintance, are the only realities we ever directly know, and the whole history of our thought is the history of our substitution of one of them for another, and the reduction of the substitute to the status of a conceptual sign. Contemned though they be by some thinkers, these sensations are the mother-earth, the anchorage, the stable rock, the first and last limits, the *terminus a quo* and the *terminus ad quem* of the mind. To find such sensational *termini* should be our aim with all our higher thought. They end discussion; they destroy the false conceit of knowledge; and without them we are all at sea with each other's meaning. If two men act alike on a percept, they believe themselves to feel alike about it; if not, they may suspect they know it in differing ways. We can never be sure we understand each other till we are able to bring the matter to this test.[1] This is why metaphysical discussions are so much like fighting with the air; they have no practical issue of a sensational kind. 'Scientific' theories, on the other hand, always terminate in definite percepts. You can deduce a possible sensation from your theory and, taking me into your laboratory, prove that your theory is true of my world by giving me the sensation then and there. Beautiful is the flight of conceptual reason through the upper air of truth. No wonder philosophers are dazzled by it still, and no wonder they look with some disdain at the low earth of feeling from which the god-

[1] 'There is no distinction of meaning so fine as to consist in anything but a possible difference of practice. . . . It appears, then, that the rule for attaining the [highest] grade of clearness of apprehension is as follows: Consider what effects, which might conceivably have practical bearings, we conceive the object of our conception to have. Then, our conception of these effects is the whole of our conception of the object.' Charles S. Peirce: 'How to make our Ideas clear,' in *Popular Science Monthly*, New York, January, 1878, p. 293.

dess launched herself aloft. But woe to her if she return not home to its acquaintance; *Nirgends haften dann die unsicheren Sohlen* — every crazy wind will take her, and, like a fire-balloon at night, she will go out among the stars.

NOTE. — The reader will easily see how much of the account of the truth-function developed later in *Pragmatism* was already explicit in this earlier article, and how much came to be defined later. In this earlier article we find distinctly asserted : —

1. The reality, external to the true idea;

2. The critic, reader, or epistemologist, with his own belief, as warrant for this reality's existence;

3. The experienceable environment, as the vehicle or medium connecting knower with known, and yielding the cognitive *relation;*

4. The notion of *pointing*, through this medium, to the reality, as one condition of our being said to know it;

5. That of *resembling* it, and eventually *affecting* it, as determining the pointing to *it* and not to something else.

6. The elimination of the 'epistemological gulf,' so that the whole truth-relation falls inside of the continuities of concrete experience, and is constituted of particular processes, varying with every object and subject, and susceptible of being described in detail.

The defects in this earlier account are : —

1. The possibly undue prominence given to resembling, which altho a fundamental function in knowing truly, is so often dispensed with;

2. The undue emphasis laid upon operating on the object itself, which in many cases is indeed decisive of that being what we refer to, but which is often lacking, or replaced by operations on other things related to the object.

3. The imperfect development of the generalized notion of the *workability* of the feeling or idea as equivalent to that *satisfactory adaptation* to the particular reality, which constitutes the truth of the idea. It is this more generalized notion, as covering all such specifications as pointing, fitting, operating or resembling, that distinguishes the developed view of Dewey, Schiller, and myself.

4. The treatment, on page 39, of percepts as the only realm of reality. I now treat concepts as a co-ordinate realm.

The next paper represents a somewhat broader grasp of the topic on the writer's part.

II

THE TIGERS IN INDIA[1]

THERE are two ways of knowing things, knowing them immediately or intuitively, and knowing them conceptually or representatively. Altho such things as the white paper before our eyes can be known intuitively, most of the things we know, the tigers now in India, for example, or the scholastic system of philosophy, are known only representatively or symbolically.

Suppose, to fix our ideas, that we take first a case of conceptual knowledge; and let it be our knowledge of the tigers in India, as we sit here. Exactly what do we *mean* by saying that we here know the tigers? What is the precise fact that the cognition so confidently claimed is *known-as*, to use Shadworth Hodgson's inelegant but valuable form of words?

Most men would answer that what we mean

---

[1] Extracts from a presidential address before the American Psychological Association, published in the *Psychological Review*, vol. ii, p. 105 (1895).

by knowing the tigers is having them, however absent in body, become in some way present to our thought; or that our knowledge of them is known as presence of our thought to them. A great mystery is usually made of this peculiar presence in absence; and the scholastic philosophy, which is only common sense grown pedantic, would explain it as a peculiar kind of existence, called *intentional inexistence*, of the tigers in our mind. At the very least, people would say that what we mean by knowing the tigers is mentally *pointing* towards them as we sit here.

But now what do we mean by *pointing*, in such a case as this? What is the pointing known-as, here?

To this question I shall have to give a very prosaic answer — one that traverses the prepossessions not only of common sense and scholasticism, but also those of nearly all the epistemological writers whom I have ever read. The answer, made brief, is this: The pointing of our thought to the tigers is known simply and solely as a procession of mental associates and motor consequences that follow on the thought, and that would lead harmoniously, if followed out, into some ideal or real context, or even into the immediate presence, of the tigers. It is known as our rejection of a jaguar, if that beast were shown us as a tiger; as our assent to a genuine tiger if so shown. It is known as our ability to utter all sorts of propositions which don't contradict other propositions that are true of the real tigers. It is even known, if we take the tigers very seriously, as actions of ours which may terminate in directly intuited tigers, as they would if we took a voyage to India for the purpose of tiger-hunting and brought back a lot of skins of the striped rascals which we had laid low. In all this there is no self-transcendency in our mental images *taken by themselves*. They are one phenomenal fact; the tigers are another; and their pointing to the tigers is a perfectly commonplace intra-experiential relation, *if you once grant a connecting world to be there*. In short, the ideas and the tigers are in themselves as loose and separate, to use

Hume's language, as any two things can be; and pointing means here an operation as external and adventitious as any that nature yields.[1]

I hope you may agree with me now that in representative knowledge there is no special inner mystery, but only an outer chain of physical or mental intermediaries connecting thought and thing. *To know an object is here to lead to it through a context which the world supplies.* All this was most instructively set forth by our colleague D. S. Miller at our meeting in New York last Christmas, and for re-confirming my sometime wavering opinion, I owe him this acknowledgment.[2]

Let us next pass on to the case of immediate

[1] A stone in one field may 'fit,' we say, a hole in another field. But the relation of 'fitting,' so long as no one carries the stone to the hole and drops it in, is only one name for the fact that such an act *may* happen. Similarly with the knowing of the tigers here and now. It is only an anticipatory name for a further associative and terminative process that *may* occur.

[2] See Dr. Miller's articles on Truth and Error, and on Content and Function, in the *Philosophical Review*, July, 1893, and Nov., 1895.

or intuitive acquaintance with an object, and let the object be the white paper before our eyes. The thought-stuff and the thing-stuff are here indistinguishably the same in nature, as we saw a moment since, and there is no context of intermediaries or associates to stand between and separate the thought and thing. There is no 'presence in absence' here, and no 'pointing,' but rather an allround embracing of the paper by the thought; and it is clear that the knowing cannot now be explained exactly as it was when the tigers were its object. Dotted all through our experience are states of immediate acquaintance just like this. Somewhere our belief always does rest on ultimate data like the whiteness, smoothness, or squareness of this paper. Whether such qualities be truly ultimate aspects of being, or only provisional suppositions of ours, held-to till we get better informed, is quite immaterial for our present inquiry. So long as it is believed in, we see our object face to face. What now do we mean by 'knowing' such a sort of object as this? For this is also the way in which we

should know the tiger if our conceptual idea
of him were to terminate by having led us to
his lair?

This address must not become too long, so I
must give my answer in the fewest words. And
let me first say this: So far as the white paper
or other ultimate datum of our experience is
considered to enter also into some one else's
experience, and we, in knowing it, are held to
know it there as well as here; so far, again, as
it is considered to be a mere mask for hidden
molecules that other now impossible experiences of our own might some day lay bare to
view; so far it is a case of tigers in India again
— the things known being absent experiences,
the knowing can only consist in passing
smoothly towards them through the intermediary context that the world supplies. But
if our own private vision of the paper be considered in abstraction from every other event,
as if it constituted by itself the universe (and
it might perfectly well do so, for aught we can
understand to the contrary), then the paper
seen and the seeing of it are only two names for

one indivisible fact which, properly named,
is *the datum, the phenomenon, or the experience*. The paper is in the mind and the mind
is around the paper, because paper and mind
are only two names that are given later to the
one experience, when, taken in a larger world
of which it forms a part, its connections
are traced in different directions.[1] *To know*

---

[1] What is meant by this is that 'the experience' can be referred to either of two great associative systems, that of the
experiencer's mental history, or that of the experienced facts
of the world. Of both of these systems it forms part, and may
be regarded, indeed, as one of their points of intersection. One
might let a vertical line stand for the mental history; but the

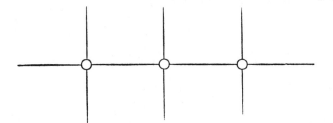

same object, O, appears also in the mental history of different
persons, represented by the other vertical lines. It thus ceases
to be the private property of one experience, and becomes, so
to speak, a shared or public thing. We can track its outer history in this way, and represent it by the horizontal line. [It
is also known representatively at other points of the vertical
lines, or intuitively there again, so that the line of its outer history would have to be looped and wandering, but I make it

immediately, then, or intuitively, is for mental content and object to be identical. This is a very different definition from that which we gave of representative knowledge; but neither definition involves those mysterious notions of self-transcendency and presence in absence which are such essential parts of the ideas of knowledge, both of philosophers and of common men.[1]

straight for simplicity's sake.] In any case, however, it is the same *stuff* that figures in all the sets of lines.

[1] [The reader will observe that the text is written from the point of view of *naïf* realism or common sense, and avoids raising the idealistic controversy.]

III

HUMANISM AND TRUTH[1]

RECEIVING from the Editor of *Mind* an advance proof of Mr. Bradley's article on 'Truth and Practice,' I understand this as a hint to me to join in the controversy over 'Pragmatism' which seems to have seriously begun. As my name has been coupled with the movement, I deem it wise to take the hint, the more so as in some quarters greater credit has been given me than I deserve, and probably undeserved discredit in other quarters falls also to my lot.

First, as to the word 'pragmatism.' I myself have only used the term to indicate a method of carrying on abstract discussion. The serious meaning of a concept, says Mr. Peirce, lies in the concrete difference to some one which its being true will make. Strive

---

[1] Reprinted, with slight verbal revision, from *Mind*, vol. xiii, N. S., p. 457 (October, 1904). A couple of interpolations from another article in *Mind*, 'Humanism and truth once more,' in vol. xiv, have been made.

to bring all debated conceptions to that 'pragmatic' test, and you will escape vain wrangling:
if it can make no practical difference which of
two statements be true, then they are really one
statement in two verbal forms; if it can make
no practical difference whether a given statement be true or false, then the statement has
no real meaning. In neither case is there
anything fit to quarrel about: we may save
our breath, and pass to more important
things.

All that the pragmatic method implies,
then, is that truths should *have* practical [1]
consequences. In England the word has been
used more broadly still, to cover the notion
that the truth of any statement *consists* in the
consequences, and particularly in their being
good consequences. Here we get beyond
affairs of method altogether; and since my
pragmatism and this wider pragmatism are so
different, and both are important enough to

---

[1] ['Practical' in the sense of *particular*, of course, not in
the sense that the consequences may not be *mental* as well
as physical.]

have different names, I think that Mr. Schiller's proposal to call the wider pragmatism by the name of 'humanism' is excellent and ought to be adopted. The narrower pragmatism may still be spoken of as the 'pragmatic method.'

I have read in the past six months many hostile reviews of Schiller's and Dewey's publications; but with the exception of Mr. Bradley's elaborate indictment, they are out of reach where I write, and I have largely forgotten them. I think that a free discussion of the subject on my part would in any case be more useful than a polemic attempt at rebutting these criticisms in detail. Mr. Bradley in particular can be taken care of by Mr. Schiller. He repeatedly confesses himself unable to comprehend Schiller's views, he evidently has not sought to do so sympathetically, and I deeply regret to say that his laborious article throws, for my mind, absolutely no useful light upon the subject. It seems to me on the whole an *ignoratio elenchi*, and I feel free to disregard it altogether.

The subject is unquestionably difficult. Messrs. Dewey's and Schiller's thought is eminently an induction, a generalization working itself free from all sorts of entangling particulars. If true, it involves much restatement of traditional notions. This is a kind of intellectual product that never attains a classic form of expression when first promulgated. The critic ought therefore not to be too sharp and logic-chopping in his dealings with it, but should weigh it as a whole, and especially weigh it against its possible alternatives. One should also try to apply it first to one instance, and then to another to see how it will work. It seems to me that it is emphatically not a case for instant execution, by conviction of intrinsic absurdity or of self-contradiction, or by caricature of what it would look like if reduced to skeleton shape. Humanism is in fact much more like one of those secular changes that come upon public opinion overnight, as it were, borne upon tides 'too deep for sound or foam,' that survive all the crudities and extravagances of their advocates, that you can pin to no one

absolutely essential statement, nor kill by any
one decisive stab.

Such have been the changes from aristocracy
to democracy, from classic to romantic taste,
from theistic to pantheistic feeling, from static
to evolutionary ways of understanding life —
changes of which we all have been spectators.
Scholasticism still opposes to such changes the
method of confutation by single decisive reasons, showing that the new view involves self-
contradiction, or traverses some fundamental
principle. This is like stopping a river by plant-
ing a stick in the middle of its bed. Round
your obstacle flows the water and 'gets there
all the same.' In reading some of our opponents, I am not a little reminded of those catholic writers who refute darwinism by telling us
that higher species cannot come from lower
because *minus nequit gignere plus*, or that the
notion of transformation is absurd, for it implies that species tend to their own destruction,
and that would violate the principle that every
reality tends to persevere in its own shape.
The point of view is too myopic, too tight and

close to take in the inductive argument. Wide
generalizations in science always meet with
these summary refutations in their early days;
but they outlive them, and the refutations then
sound oddly antiquated and scholastic. I cannot help suspecting that the humanistic theory
is going through this kind of would-be refutation at present.

The one condition of understanding humanism is to become inductive-minded oneself, to
drop rigorous definitions, and follow lines of
least resistance 'on the whole.' 'In other
words,' an opponent might say, 'resolve your
intellect into a kind of slush.' 'Even so,' I
make reply, — 'if you will consent to use no
politer word.' For humanism, conceiving the
more 'true' as the more 'satisfactory' (Dewey's
term), has sincerely to renounce rectilinear arguments and ancient ideals of rigor and final-
ity. It is in just this temper of renunciation, so
different from that of pyrrhonistic scepticism,
that the spirit of humanism essentially consists.
Satisfactoriness has to be measured by a mul-
titude of standards, of which some, for aught

we know, may fail in any given case; and what is more satisfactory than any alternative in sight, may to the end be a sum of *pluses* and *minuses*, concerning which we can only trust that by ulterior corrections and improvements a maximum of the one and a minimum of the other may some day be approached. It means a real change of heart, a break with absolutistic hopes, when one takes up this inductive view of the conditions of belief.

As I understand the pragmatist way of seeing things, it owes its being to the break-down which the last fifty years have brought about in the older notions of scientific truth. 'God geometrizes,' it used to be said; and it was believed that Euclid's elements literally reproduced his geometrizing. There is an eternal and unchangeable 'reason'; and its voice was supposed to reverberate in *Barbara* and *Celarent*. So also of the 'laws of nature,' physical and chemical, so of natural history classifications — all were supposed to be exact and exclusive duplicates of pre-human archetypes buried in the structure of things, to which the spark of divinity hidden in our intellect enables us to penetrate. The anatomy of the world is logical, and its logic is that of a university professor, it was thought. Up to about 1850 almost every one believed that sciences expressed truths that were exact copies of a definite code of non-human realities. But the enormously rapid multiplication of theories in these latter days has well-nigh upset the notion of any one of them being a more literally objective kind of thing than another. There are so many geometries, so many logics, so many physical and chemical hypotheses, so many classifications, each one of them good for so much and yet not good for everything, that the notion that even the truest formula may be a human device and not a literal transcript has dawned upon us. We hear scientific laws now treated as so much 'conceptual shorthand,' true so far as they are useful but no farther. Our mind has become tolerant of symbol instead of reproduction, of approximation instead of exactness, of plasticity instead of rigor. 'Energetics,' measuring the bare face of sensible phenomena so as to describe in a single formula all their changes of 'level,' is the last word of this scientific humanism, which indeed leaves queries enough outstanding as to the reason for so curious a congruence between the world and the mind, but which at any rate makes our whole notion of scientific truth more flexible and genial than it used to be.

It is to be doubted whether any theorizer to-day, either in mathematics, logic, physics or biology, conceives himself to be literally re-editing processes of nature or thoughts of God. The main forms of our thinking, the separation of subjects from predicates, the negative, hypothetic' and disjunctive judgments, are purely human habits. The ether, as Lord Salisbury said, is only a noun for the verb to undulate; and many of our theological ideas are admitted, even by those who call them 'true,' to be humanistic in like degree.

I fancy that these changes in the current notions of truth are what criginally gave the impulse to Messrs. Dewey's and Schiller's

views. The suspicion is in the air nowadays
that the superiority of one of our formulas to
another may not consist so much in its literal
'objectivity,' as in subjective qualities like its
usefulness, its 'elegance' or its congruity with
our residual beliefs. Yielding to these suspi-
cions, and generalizing, we fall into something
like the humanistic state of mind. Truth we
conceive to mean everywhere, not duplication,
but addition; not the constructing of inner
copies of already complete realities, but rather
the collaborating with realities so as to
bring about a clearer result. Obviously this
state of mind is at first full of vagueness and
ambiguity. 'Collaborating' is a vague term; it
must at any rate cover conceptions and logical
arrangements. 'Clearer' is vaguer still. Truth
must bring clear thoughts, as well as clear the
way to action. 'Reality' is the vaguest term
of all. The only way to test such a programme
at all is to apply it to the various types of truth,
in the hope of reaching an account that shall
be more precise. Any hypothesis that forces
such a review upon one has one great merit,

even if in the end it prove invalid: it gets us better acquainted with the total subject. To give the theory plenty of 'rope' and see if it hangs itself eventually is better tactics than to choke it off at the outset by abstract accusations of self-contradiction. I think therefore that a decided effort at sympathetic mental play with humanism is the provisional attitude to be recommended to the reader.

When I find myself playing sympathetically with humanism, something like what follows is what I end by conceiving it to mean.

Experience is a process that continually gives us new material to digest. We handle this intellectually by the mass of beliefs of which we find ourselves already possessed, assimilating, rejecting, or rearranging in different degrees. Some of the apperceiving ideas are recent acquisitions of our own, but most of them are common-sense traditions of the race. There is probably not a common-sense tradition, of all those which we now live by, that was not in the first instance a genuine discovery, an inductive generalization like those more recent ones of the atom, of inertia, of energy, of reflex action, or of fitness to survive. The notions of one Time and of one Space as single continuous receptacles; the distinction between thoughts and things, matter and mind; between permanent subjects and changing attributes; the conception of classes with subclasses within them; the separation of fortuitous from regularly caused connections; surely all these were once definite conquests made at historic dates by our ancestors in their attempts to get the chaos of their crude individual experiences into a more shareable and manageable shape. They proved of such sovereign use as *denkmittel* that they are now a part of the very structure of our mind. We cannot play fast and loose with them. No experience can upset them. On the contrary, they apperceive every experience and assign it to its place.

To what effect? That we may the better foresee the course of our experiences, communicate with one another, and steer our lives by rule. Also that we may have a cleaner, clearer, more inclusive mental view.

The greatest common-sense achievement, after the discovery of one Time and one Space, is probably the concept of permanently existing things. When a rattle first drops out of the hand of a baby, he does not look to see where it has gone. Non-perception he accepts as annihilation until he finds a better belief. That our perceptions mean *beings*, rattles that are there whether we hold them in our hands or not, becomes an interpretation so luminous of what happens to us that, once employed, it never gets forgotten. It applies with equal felicity to things and persons, to the objective and to the ejective realm. However a Berkeley, a Mill, or a Cornelius may criticise it, it *works;* and in practical life we never think of 'going back' upon it, or reading our incoming experiences in any other terms. We may, indeed, speculatively imagine a state of 'pure' experience before the hypothesis of permanent objects behind its flux had been framed; and we can play with the idea that some primeval

genius might have struck into a different hypothesis. But we cannot positively imagine to-
day what the different hypothesis could have
been, for the category of trans-perceptual reality is now one of the foundations of our life.
Our thoughts must still employ it if they are
to possess reasonableness and truth.

This notion of a *first* in the shape of a most
chaotic pure experience which sets us questions, of a *second* in the way of fundamental
categories, long ago wrought into the structure
of our consciousness and practically irreversible, which define the general frame within
which answers must fall, and of a *third* which
gives the detail of the answers in the shapes
most congruous with all our present needs, is,
as I take it, the essence of the humanistic conception. It represents experience in its pristine
purity to be now so enveloped in predicates
historically worked out that we can think of
it as little more than an *Other*, of a *That*, which
the mind, in Mr. Bradley's phrase, 'encoun-
ters,' and to whose stimulating presence we
respond by ways of thinking which we call

'true' in proportion as they facilitate our mental or physical activities and bring us outer power and inner peace. But whether the Other, the universal *That*, has itself any definite inner structure, or whether, if it have any, the structure resembles any of our predicated *whats*, this is a question which humanism leaves untouched. For us, at any rate, it insists, reality is an accumulation of our own intellectual inventions, and the struggle for 'truth' in our progressive dealings with it is always a struggle to work in new nouns and adjectives while altering as little as possible the old.

It is hard to see why either Mr. Bradley's own logic or his metaphysics should oblige him to quarrel with this conception. He might consistently adopt it *verbatim et literatim*, if he would, and simply throw his peculiar absolute round it, following in this the good example of Professor Royce. Bergson in France, and his disciples, Wilbois the physicist and Leroy, are thoroughgoing humanists in the sense defined. Professor Milhaud also appears to be one; and the great Poincaré misses it by only the breadth of a hair. In Germany the name of Simmel offers itself as that of a humanist of the most radical sort. Mach and his school, and Hertz and Ostwald must be classed as humanists. The view is in the atmosphere and must be patiently discussed.

The best way to discuss it would be to see what the alternative might be. What is it indeed? Its critics make no explicit statement, Professor Royce being the only one so far who has formulated anything definite. The first service of humanism to philosophy accordingly seems to be that it will probably oblige those who dislike it to search their own hearts and heads. It will force analysis to the front and make it the order of the day. At present the lazy tradition that truth is *adæquatio intellectûs et rei* seems all there is to contradict it with. Mr. Bradley's only suggestion is that true thought 'must correspond to a determinate being which it cannot be said to make,' and obviously that sheds no new light. What is the meaning of the word to 'correspond'? Where is the 'being'? What sort of things are 'determinations,' and what is meant in this particular case by 'not to make'?

Humanism proceeds immediately to refine upon the looseness of these epithets. We correspond in *some* way with anything with which we enter into any relations at all. If it be a thing, we may produce an exact copy of it, or we may simply feel it as an existent in a certain place. If it be a demand, we may obey it without knowing anything more about it than its push. If it be a proposition, we may agree by not contradicting it, by letting it pass. If it be a relation between things, we may act on the first thing so as to bring ourselves out where the second will be. If it be something inaccessible, we may substitute a hypothetical object for it, which, having the same consequences, will cipher out for us real results. In a general way we may simply *add our thought to it;* and if it *suffers the addition,* and the whole situation harmoniously prolongs and enriches itself, the thought will pass for true.

As for the whereabouts of the beings thus corresponded to, although they may be outside of the present thought as well as in it, humanism sees no ground for saying they are outside of finite experience itself. Pragmatically, their reality means that we submit to them, take account of them, whether we like to or not, but this we must perpetually do with experiences other than our own. The whole system of what the present experience must correspond to 'adequately' may be continuous with the present experience itself. Reality, so taken as experience other than the present, might be either the legacy of past experience or the content of experience to come. Its determinations for *us* are in any case the adjectives which our acts of judging fit to it, and those are essentially humanistic things.

To say that our thought does not 'make' this reality means pragmatically that if our own particular thought were annihilated the reality would still be there in some shape, though possibly it might be a shape that would lack something that our thought supplies.

That reality is 'independent' means that there is something in every experience that escapes our arbitrary control. If it be a sensible experience it coerces our attention; if a sequence, we cannot invert it; if we compare two terms we can come to only one result. There is a push, an urgency, within our very experience, against which we are on the whole powerless, and which drives us in a direction that is the destiny of our belief. That this drift of experience itself is in the last resort due to something independent of all possible experience may or may not be true. There may or may not be an extra-experiential 'ding an sich' that keeps the ball rolling, or an 'absolute' that lies eternally behind all the successive determinations which human thought has made. But within our experience *itself*, at any rate, humanism says, some determinations show themselves as being independent of others; some questions, if we ever ask them, can only be answered in one way; some beings, if we ever suppose them, must be supposed to have existed previously to the supposing; some relations, if they exist ever, must exist as long as their terms exist.

Truth thus means, according to humanism, the relation of less fixed parts of experience (predicates) to other relatively more fixed parts (subjects); and we are not required to seek it in a relation of experience as such to anything beyond itself. We can stay at home, for our behavior as experients is hemmed in on every side. The forces both of advance and of resistance are exerted by our own objects, and the notion of truth as something opposed to waywardness or license inevitably grows up solipsistically inside of every human life.

So obvious is all this that a common charge against the humanistic authors 'makes me tired.' 'How can a deweyite discriminate sincerity from bluff?' was a question asked at a philosophic meeting where I reported on Dewey's *Studies.* 'How can the mere [1] prag-

[1] I know of no 'mere' pragmatist, if *mereness* here means, as it seems to, the denial of all concreteness to the pragmatist's thought.

matist feel any duty to think truly?' is the objection urged by Professor Royce. Mr. Bradley in turn says that if a humanist understands his own doctrine, 'he must hold any idea, however mad, to be the truth, if any one will have it so.' And Professor Taylor describes pragmatism as believing anything one pleases and calling it truth.

Such a shallow sense of the conditions under which men's thinking actually goes on seems to me most surprising. These critics appear to suppose that, if left to itself, the rudderless raft of our experience must be ready to drift anywhere or nowhere. Even tho there were compasses on board, they seem to say, there would be no pole for them to point to. There must be absolute sailing-directions, they insist, decreed from outside, and an independent chart of the voyage added to the 'mere' voyage itself, if we are ever to make a port. But is it not obvious that even tho there be such absolute sailing-directions in the shape of pre-human standards of truth that we *ought* to follow, the only guarantee that we shall in fact follow them must lie in our human equipment. The 'ought' would be a *brutum fulmen* unless there were a felt grain inside of our experience that conspired. As a matter of fact the devoutest believers in absolute standards must admit that men fail to obey them. Waywardness is here, in spite of the eternal prohibitions, and the existence of any amount of reality *ante rem* is no warrant against unlimited error *in rebus* being incurred. The only *real* guarantee we have against licentious thinking is the circumpressure of experience itself, which gets us sick of concrete errors, whether there be a trans-empirical reality or not. How does the partisan of absolute reality know what this orders him to think? He cannot get direct sight of the absolute; and he has no means of guessing what it wants of him except by following the humanistic clues. The only truth that he himself will ever practically *accept* will be that to which his finite experiences lead him of themselves. The state of mind which shudders at the idea of a lot of experiences left to themselves, and that augurs protection from the sheer name of an absolute, as if, however inoperative, that might still stand for a sort of ghostly security, is like the mood of those good people who, whenever they hear of a social tendency that is damnable, begin to redden and to puff, and say 'Parliament or Congress ought to make a law against it,' as if an impotent decree would give relief.

All the *sanctions* of a law of truth lie in the very texture of experience. Absolute or no absolute, the concrete truth *for us* will always be that way of thinking in which our various experiences most profitably combine.

And yet, the opponent obstinately urges, your humanist will always have a greater liberty to play fast and loose with truth than will your believer in an independent realm of reality that makes the standard rigid. If by this latter believer he means a man who pretends to know the standard and who fulminates it, the humanist will doubtless prove more flexible; but no more flexible than the absolutist himself if the latter follows (as fortunately our present-day absolutists do follow) empirical methods of inquiry in concrete affairs. To consider hypotheses is surely always better than to dogmatize *ins blaue hinein.*

Nevertheless this probable flexibility of temper in him has been used to convict the humanist of sin. Believing as he does, that truth lies *in rebus,* and is at every moment our own line of most propitious reaction, he stands forever debarred, as I have heard a learned colleague say, from trying to convert opponents, for does not their view, being *their* most propitious momentary reaction, already fill the bill? Only the believer in the *ante-rem* brand of truth can on this theory seek to make converts without self-stultification. But can there be self-stultification in urging any account whatever of truth? Can the definition ever contradict the deed? 'Truth is what I feel like saying' — suppose that to be the definition. 'Well, I feel like saying that, and I want you to feel like saying it, and shall continue to say it until I get you to agree.' Where is there any contradiction? Whatever truth may be said

to be, that is the kind of truth which the saying can be held to carry. The *temper* which a
saying may comport is an extra-logical matter.
It may indeed be hotter in some individual
absolutist than in a humanist, but it need not
be so in another. And the humanist, for his
part, is perfectly consistent in compassing sea
and land to make one proselyte, if his nature
be enthusiastic enough.

'But how *can* you be enthusiastic over any
view of things which you know to have been
partly made by yourself, and which is liable
to alter during the next minute? How is any
heroic devotion to the ideal of truth possible
under such paltry conditions?'

This is just another of those objections by
which the anti-humanists show their own com-
paratively slack hold on the realities of the
situation. If they would only follow the pragmatic method and ask : 'What is truth *known-
as?* What does its existence stand for in the
way of concrete goods?' — they would see
that the name of it is the *inbegriff* of almost
everything that is valuable in our lives. The

true is the opposite of whatever is instable, of whatever is practically disappointing, of whatever is useless, of whatever is lying and unreliable, of whatever is unverifiable and unsupported, of whatever is inconsistent and contradictory, of whatever is artificial and eccentric, of whatever is unreal in the sense of being of no practical account. Here are pragmatic reasons with a vengeance why we should turn to truth — truth saves us from a world of that complexion. What wonder that its very name awakens loyal feeling! In particular what wonder that all little provisional fool's paradises of belief should appear contemptible in comparison with its bare pursuit! When absolutists reject humanism because they feel it to be untrue, that means that the whole habit of their mental needs is wedded already to a different view of reality, in comparison with which the humanistic world seems but the whim of a few irresponsible youths. Their own subjective apperceiving mass is what speaks here in the name of the eternal natures and bids them reject our humanism — as they apprehend it. Just so with us humanists, when we condemn all noble, clean-cut, fixed, eternal, rational, temple-like systems of philosophy. These contradict the *dramatic temperament* of nature, as our dealings with nature and our habits of thinking have so far brought us to conceive it. They seem oddly personal and artificial, even when not bureaucratic and professional in an absurd degree. We turn from them to the great unpent and unstayed wilderness of truth as we feel it to be constituted, with as good a conscience as rationalists are moved by when they turn from our wilderness into their neater and cleaner intellectual abodes.[1]

[1] [I cannot forbear quoting as an illustration of the contrast between humanist and rationalist tempers of mind, in a sphere remote from philosophy, these remarks on the Dreyfus 'affaire,' written by one who assuredly had never heard of humanism or pragmatism. 'Autant que la Révolution, "l'Affaire" est désormais une de nos "origines." Si elle n'a pas fait ouvrir le gouffre, c'est elle du moins qui a rendu patent et visible le long travail souterrain qui, silencieusement, avait preparé la séparation entre nos deux camps d'aujourd'hui, pour écarter enfin, d'un coup soudain, *la France des traditionalistes (poseurs de principes, chercheurs d'unité, constructeurs de systèmes à priori) et la France éprise*

This is surely enough to show that the humanist does not ignore the character of objectivity and independence in truth. Let me turn next to what his opponents mean when they say that to be true, our thoughts must 'correspond.'

The vulgar notion of correspondence here is that the thoughts must *copy* the reality — cognitio fit per *assimiliationem* cogniti et cognoscentis; and philosophy, without having ever fairly sat down to the question, seems to have instinctively accepted this idea: propositions are held true if they copy the eternal thought; terms are held true if they copy extra-mental

du fait positif et de libre examen; — la France révolutionnaire et romantique si l'on veut, celle qui met très haut l'individu, qui ne veut pas qu'un juste périsse, fut-ce pour sauver la nation, et qui cherche la vérité dans toutes ses parties aussi bien que dans une vue d'ensemble. . . . Duclaux ne pouvait pas concevoir qu'on préférât quelque chose à la vérité. Mais il voyait autour de lui de fort honnêtes gens qui, mettant en balance la vie d'un homme et la raison d'État, lui avouaient de quel poids léger ils jugeaient une simple existence individuelle, pour innocente qu'elle fût. *C'etaient des classiques, des gens à qui l'ensemble seul importe.*' *La Vie de Emile Duclaux,* par Mme. Em. D., Laval, 1906, pp. 243, 247–248.]

realities. Implicitly, I think that the copy-theory has animated most of the criticisms that have been made on humanism.

A priori, however, it is not self-evident that the sole business of our mind with realities should be to copy them. Let my reader suppose himself to constitute for a time all the reality there is in the universe, and then to receive the announcement that another being is to be created who shall know him truly. How will he represent the knowing in advance? What will he hope it to be? I doubt extremely whether it could ever occur to him to fancy it as a mere copying. Of what use to him would an imperfect second edition of himself in the new comer's interior be? It would seem pure waste of a propitious opportunity. The demand would more probably be for something absolutely new. The reader would conceive the knowing humanistically, 'the new comer,' he would say, ' must *take account of my presence by reacting on it in such a way that good would accrue to us both.* If copying be requisite to that end, let there be copying; otherwise not.'

The essence in any case would not be the copying, but the enrichment of the previous world.

I read the other day, in a book of Professor Eucken's, a phrase, '*Die erhöhung des vorgefundenen daseins,*' which seems to be pertinent here. Why may not thought's mission be to increase and elevate, rather than simply to imitate and reduplicate, existence? No one who has read Lotze can fail to remember his striking comment on the ordinary view of the secondary qualities of matter, which brands them as 'illusory' because they copy nothing in the thing. The notion of a world complete in itself, to which thought comes as a passive mirror, adding nothing to fact, Lotze says is irrational. Rather is thought itself a most momentous part of fact, and the whole mission of the pre-existing and insufficient world of matter may simply be to provoke thought to produce its far more precious supplement.

'Knowing,' in short, may, for aught we can see beforehand to the contrary, be *only one way of getting into fruitful relations with real-*

ity, whether copying be one of the relations or not.

It is easy to see from what special type of knowing the copy-theory arose. In our dealings with natural phenomena the great point is to be able to foretell. Foretelling, according to such a writer as Spencer, is the whole meaning of intelligence. When Spencer's 'law of intelligence' says that inner and outer relations must 'correspond,' it means that the distribution of terms in our inner time-scheme and space-scheme must be an exact copy of the distribution in real time and space of the real terms. In strict theory the mental terms themselves need not answer to the real terms in the sense of severally copying them, symbolic mental terms being enough, if only the real dates and places be copied. But in our ordinary life the mental terms are images and the real ones are sensations, and the images so often copy the sensations, that we easily take copying of terms as well as of relations to be the natural significance of knowing. Meanwhile much, even of this common descriptive truth, is couched in verbal symbols. If our symbols *fit* the world, in the sense of determining our expectations rightly, they may even be the better for not copying its terms.

It seems obvious that the pragmatic account of all this routine of phenomenal knowledge is accurate. Truth here is a relation, not of our ideas to non-human realities, but of conceptual parts of our experience to sensational parts. Those thoughts are true which guide us to *beneficial interaction* with sensible particulars as they occur, whether they copy these in advance or not.

From the frequency of copying in the knowledge of phenomenal fact, copying has been supposed to be the essence of truth in matters rational also. Geometry and logic, it has been supposed, must copy archetypal thoughts in the Creator. But in these abstract spheres there is no need of assuming archetypes. The mind is free to carve so many figures out of space, to make so many numerical collections, to frame so many classes and series, and it can analyze and compare so endlessly, that the very superabundance of the resulting ideas makes us doubt the 'objective' pre-existence of their models. It would be plainly wrong to suppose a God whose thought consecrated rectangular but not polar co-ordinates, or Jevons's notation but not Boole's. Yet if, on the other hand, we assume God to have thought in advance of every *possible* flight of human fancy in these directions, his mind becomes too much like a Hindoo idol with three heads, eight arms and six breasts, too much made up of superfœtation and redundancy for us to wish to copy it, and the whole notion of copying tends to evaporate from these sciences. Their objects can be better interpreted as being created step by step by men, as fast as they successively conceive them.

If now it be asked how, if triangles, squares, square roots, genera, and the like, are but improvised human 'artefacts,' their properties and relations can be so promptly known to be 'eternal,' the humanistic answer is easy. If triangles and genera are of our own production we can keep them invariant. We can

make them 'timeless' by expressly decreeing
that on *the things we mean* time shall exert
no altering effect, that they are intentionally
and it may be fictitiously abstracted from every
corrupting real associate and condition. But
relations between invariant objects will themselves be invariant. Such relations cannot be
happenings, for by hypothesis nothing shall
happen to the objects. I have tried to show
in the last chapter of my *Principles of Psychology*[1] that they can only be relations of
comparison. No one so far seems to have noticed my suggestion, and I am too ignorant of
the development of mathematics to feel very
confident of my own view. But if it were
correct it would solve the difficulty perfectly.
Relations of comparison are matters of direct
inspection. As soon as mental objects are
mentally compared, they are perceived to be
either like or unlike. But once the same, always the same, once different, always different,
under these timeless conditions. Which is as
much as to say that truths concerning these

[1] Vol. ii, pp. 641 ff.

man-made objects are necessary and eternal. We can change our conclusions only by changing our data first.

The whole fabric of the *a priori* sciences can thus be treated as a man-made product. As Locke long ago pointed out, these sciences have no immediate connection with fact. Only *if* a fact can be humanized by being identified with any of these ideal objects, is what was true of the objects now true also of the facts. The truth itself meanwhile was originally a copy of nothing; it was only a relation directly perceived to obtain between two artificial mental things.[1]

We may now glance at some special types of knowing, so as to see better whether the humanistic account fits. On the mathematical and logical types we need not enlarge further, nor need we return at much length to the case of our descriptive knowledge of the course of nature. So far as this involves anticipation,

[1] [Mental things which are realities of course within the mental world.]

tho that *may* mean copying, it need, as we saw, mean little more than 'getting ready' in advance. But with many distant and future objects, our practical relations are to the last degree potential and remote. In no sense can we now get ready for the arrest of the earth's revolution by the tidal brake, for instance; and with the past, tho we suppose ourselves to know it truly, we have no practical relations at all. It is obvious that, altho interests strictly practical have been the original starting-point of our search for true phenomenal descriptions, yet an intrinsic interest in the bare describing function has grown up. We wish accounts that shall be true, whether they bring collateral profit or not. The primitive function has developed its demand for mere exercise. This theoretic curiosity seems to be the characteristically human *differentia*, and humanism recognizes its enormous scope. A true idea now means not only one that prepares us for an actual perception. It means also one that might prepare us for a merely possible perception, or one that, if spoken,

would suggest possible perceptions to others,
or suggest actual perceptions which the speaker
cannot share. The *ensemble* of perceptions
thus thought of as either actual or possible
form a system which it is obviously advantageous to us to get into a stable and consistent
shape; and here it is that the common-sense
notion of permanent beings finds triumphant
use. Beings acting outside of the thinker explain, not only his actual perceptions, past and
future, but his possible perceptions and those
of every one else. Accordingly they gratify our
theoretic need in a supremely beautiful way.
We pass from our immediate actual through
them into the foreign and the potential, and
back again into the future actual, accounting
for innumerable particulars by a single cause.
As in those circular panoramas, where a real
foreground of dirt, grass, bushes, rocks and a
broken-down cannon is enveloped by a can-
vas picture of sky and earth and of a raging
battle, continuing the foreground so cunningly
that the spectator can detect no joint; so these
conceptual objects, added to our present per-

ceptual reality, fuse with it into the whole universe of our belief. In spite of all berkeleyan criticism, we do not doubt that they are really there. Tho our discovery of any one of them may only date from now, we unhesitatingly say that it not only *is*, but *was* there, if, by so saying, the past appears connected more consistently with what we feel the present to be. This is historic truth. Moses wrote the Pentateuch, we think, because if he did n't, all our religious habits will have to be undone. Julius Cæsar was real, or we can never listen to history again. Trilobites were once alive, or all our thought about the strata is at sea. Radium, discovered only yesterday, must always have existed, or its analogy with other natural elements, which are permanent, fails. In all this, it is but one portion of our beliefs reacting on another so as to yield the most satisfactory total state of mind. That state of mind, we say, sees truth, and the content of its deliverances we believe.

Of course, if you take the satisfactoriness concretely, as something felt by you now, and if, by truth, you mean truth taken abstractly and verified in the long run, you cannot make them equate, for it is notorious that the temporarily satisfactory is often false. Yet at each and every concrete moment, truth for each man is what that man 'troweth' at that moment with the maximum of satisfaction to himself; and similarly, abstract truth, truth verified by the long run, and abstract satisfactoriness, long-run satisfactoriness, coincide. If, in short, we compare concrete with concrete and abstract with abstract, the true and the satisfactory do mean the same thing. I suspect that a certain muddling of matters hereabouts is what makes the general philosophic public so impervious to humanism's claims.

The fundamental fact about our experience is that it is a process of change. For the 'trower' at any moment, truth, like the visible area round a man walking in a fog, or like what George Eliot calls 'the wall of dark seen by small fishes' eyes that pierce a span in the wide Ocean,' is an objective field which the next moment enlarges and of which it is the critic, and which then either suffers alteration or is continued unchanged. The critic sees both the first trower's truth and his own truth, compares them with each other, and verifies or confutes. *His* field of view is the reality independent of that earlier trower's thinking with which that thinking ought to correspond. But the critic is himself only a trower; and if the whole process of experience should terminate at that instant, there would be no otherwise known independent reality with which *his* thought might be compared.

The immediate in experience is always provisionally in this situation. The humanism, for instance, which I see and try so hard to defend, is the completest truth attained from my point of view up to date. But, owing to the fact that all experience is a process, no point of view can ever be *the* last one. Every one is insufficient and off its balance, and responsible to later points of view than itself. You, occupying some of these later points in your own person, and believing in the reality of others, will not agree that my point of view sees truth positive, truth timeless, truth that counts, unless they verify and confirm what it sees.

You generalize this by saying that any opinion, however satisfactory, can count positively and absolutely as true only so far as it agrees with a standard beyond itself; and if you then forget that this standard perpetually grows up endogenously inside the web of the experiences, you may carelessly go on to say that what distributively holds of each experience, holds also collectively of all experience, and that experience as such and in its totality owes whatever truth it may be possessed-of to its correspondence with absolute realities outside of its own being. This evidently is the popular and traditional position. From the fact that finite experiences must draw support from one another, philosophers pass to the notion that experience *überhaupt* must need an absolute support. The denial of such a notion by humanism lies probably at the root of most of the dislike which it incurs.

But is this not the globe, the elephant and

the tortoise over again? Must not something
end by supporting itself? Humanism is willing
to let finite experience be self-supporting.
Somewhere being must immediately breast
nonentity. Why may not the advancing front
of experience, carrying its immanent satisfactions and dissatisfactions, cut against the
black inane as the luminous orb of the moon
cuts the cærulean abyss? Why should anywhere the world be absolutely fixed and fin-
ished? And if reality genuinely grows, why
may it not grow in these very determinations
which here and now are made?

In point of fact it actually seems to grow
by our mental determinations, be these never
so 'true.' Take the 'great bear' or 'dipper'
constellation in the heavens. We call it by
that name, we count the stars and call them
seven, we say they were seven before they were
counted, and we say that whether any one had
ever noted the fact or not, the dim resemblance
to a long-tailed (or long-necked?) animal was
always truly there. But what do we mean

by this projection into past eternity of recent human ways of thinking? Did an 'absolute' thinker actually do the counting, tell off the stars upon his standing number-tally, and make the bear-comparison, silly as the latter is? Were they explicitly seven, explicitly bear-like, before the human witness came? Surely nothing in the truth of the attributions drives us to think this. They were only implicitly or virtually what we call them, and we human witnesses first explicated them and made them 'real.' A fact virtually pre-exists when every condition of its realization save one is already there. In this case the condition lacking is the act of the counting and comparing mind. But the stars (once the mind considers them) themselves dictate the result. The counting in no wise modifies their previous nature, and, they being what and where they are, the count cannot fall out differently. It could then *always* be made. *Never* could the number seven be questioned, *if the question once were raised.*

We have here a quasi-paradox. Undeniably

something comes by the counting that was not there before. And yet that something was *always true*. In one sense you create it, and in another sense you *find* it. You have to treat your count as being true beforehand, the moment you come to treat the matter at all.

Our stellar attributes must always be called true, then; yet none the less are they genuine additions made by our intellect to the world of fact. Not additions of consciousness only, but additions of 'content.' They copy nothing that pre-existed, yet they agree with what pre-existed, fit it, amplify it, relate and connect it with a 'wain,' a number-tally, or what not, and build it out. It seems to me that humanism is the only theory that builds this case out in the good direction, and this case stands for innumerable other kinds of case. In all such cases, odd as it may sound, our judgment may actually be said to retroact and to enrich the past.

Our judgments at any rate change the character of *future* reality by the acts to which they

lead. Where these acts are acts expressive of
trust, — trust, *e. g.*, that a man is honest,
that our health is good enough, or that we
can make a successful effort, — which acts
may be a needed antecedent of the trusted
things becoming true, Professor Taylor says[1]
that our trust is at any rate *untrue when it is
made, i. e.*, before the action; and I seem to
remember that he disposes of anything like a
faith in the general excellence of the universe
(making the faithful person's part in it at any
rate more excellent) as a 'lie in the soul.' But
the pathos of this expression should not blind
us to the complication of the facts. I doubt
whether Professor Taylor would himself be in
favor of practically handling trusters of these
kinds as liars. Future and present really mix
in such emergencies, and one can always escape lies in them by using hypothetic forms.
But Mr. Taylor's attitude suggests such absurd possibilities of practice that it seems to

[1] In an article criticising Pragmatism (as he conceives it)
in the *McGill University Quarterly* published at Montreal,
for May, 1904.

me to illustrate beautifully how self-stultifying the conception of a truth that shall merely register a standing fixture may become. Theoretic truth, truth of passive copying, sought in the sole interests of copying as such, not because copying is *good for something*, but because copying ought *schlechthin* to be, seems, if you look at it coldly, to be an almost preposterous ideal. Why should the universe, existing in itself, also exist in copies? How *can* it be copied in the solidity of its objective fulness? And even if it could, what would the motive be? 'Even the hairs of your head are numbered.' Doubtless they are, virtually; but why, as an absolute proposition, *ought* the number to become copied and known? Surely knowing is only one way of interacting with reality and adding to its effect.

The opponent here will ask: 'Has not the knowing of truth any substantive value on its own account, apart from the collateral advantages it may bring? And if you allow theoretic satisfactions to exist at all, do they not crowd the collateral satisfactions out of house and home, and must not pragmatism go into bankruptcy, if she admits them at all?' The destructive force of such talk disappears as soon as we use words concretely instead of abstractly, and ask, in our quality of good pragmatists, just what the famous theoretic needs are known as and in what the intellectual satisfactions consist.

Are they not all mere matters of *consistency* — and emphatically *not* of consistency between an absolute reality and the mind's copies of it, but of actually felt consistency among judgments, objects, and habits of reacting, in the mind's own experienceable world? And are not both our need of such consistency and our pleasure in it conceivable as outcomes of the natural fact that we are beings that do develop mental *habits* — habit itself proving adaptively beneficial in an environment where the same objects, or the same kinds of objects, recur and follow 'law'? If this were so, what would have come first would have been the collateral profits of habit as such, and the theoretic life would have grown up in aid of these.

In point of fact, this seems to have been the probable case. At life's origin, any present perception may have been 'true' — if such a word could then be applicable. Later, when reactions became organized, the reactions became 'true' whenever expectation was fulfilled by them. Otherwise they were 'false' or 'mistaken' reactions. But the same class of objects needs the same kind of reaction, so the impulse to react consistently must gradually have been established, and a disappointment felt whenever the results frustrated expectation. Here is a perfectly plausible germ for all our higher consistencies. Nowadays, if an object claims from us a reaction of the kind habitually accorded only to the opposite class of objects, our mental machinery refuses to run smoothly. The situation is intellectually unsatisfactory.

Theoretic truth thus falls *within* the mind, being the accord of some of its processes and objects with other processes and objects — 'accord' consisting here in well-definable relations. So long as the satisfaction of feeling such an accord is denied us, whatever collateral profits may seem to inure from what we believe in are but as dust in the balance — provided always that we are highly organized intellectually, which the majority of us are not. The amount of accord which satisfies most men and women is merely the absence of violent clash between their usual thoughts and statements and the limited sphere of sense-perceptions in which their lives are cast. The theoretic truth that most of us think we 'ought' to attain to is thus the possession of a set of predicates that do not explicitly contradict their subjects. We preserve it as often as not by leaving other predicates and subjects out.

In some men theory is a passion, just as music is in others. The form of inner consistency is pursued far beyond the line at which collateral profits stop. Such men systematize and classify and schematize and make synoptical tables and invent ideal objects for the pure love of unifying. Too often the results, glowing with 'truth' for the inventors, seem pathetically personal and artificial to bystanders. Which is as much as to say that the purely

99

theoretic criterion of truth can leave us in the lurch as easily as any other criterion, and that the absolutists, for all their pretensions, are 'in the same boat' concretely with those whom they attack.

I am well aware that this paper has been rambling in the extreme. But the whole subject is inductive, and sharp logic is hardly yet in order. My great trammel has been the non-existence of any definitely stated alternative on my opponents' part. It may conduce to clearness if I recapitulate, in closing, what I conceive the main points of humanism to be. They are these : —

1. An experience, perceptual or conceptual, must conform to reality in order to be true.

2. By 'reality' humanism means nothing more than the other conceptual or perceptual experiences with which a given present experience may find itself in point of fact mixed up.[1]

---

[1] This is meant merely to exclude reality of an 'unknowable' sort, of which no account in either perceptual or conceptual terms can be given. It includes of course any amount of empirical reality independent of the knower. Pragmatism is thus 'epistemologically' realistic in its account.

3. By 'conforming,' humanism means taking account-of in such a way as to gain any intellectually and practically satisfactory result.

4. To 'take account-of' and to be 'satisfactory' are terms that admit of no definition, so many are the ways in which these requirements can practically be worked out.

5. Vaguely and in general, we take account of a reality by *preserving* it in as unmodified a form as possible. But, to be then satisfactory, it must not contradict other realities outside of it which claim also to be preserved. That we must preserve all the experience we can and minimize contradiction in what we preserve, is about all that can be said in advance.

6. The truth which the conforming experience embodies may be a positive addition to the previous reality, and later judgments may have to conform to *it*. Yet, virtually at least, it may have been true previously. Pragmatically, virtual and actual truth mean the same thing: the possibility of only one answer, *when once the question is raised.*

IV

THE RELATION BETWEEN KNOWER AND KNOWN [1]

THROUGHOUT the history of philosophy the subject and its object have been treated as absolutely discontinuous entities; and thereupon the presence of the latter to the former, or the 'apprehension' by the former of the latter, has assumed a paradoxical character which all sorts of theories had to be invented to overcome. Representative theories put a mental 'representation,' 'image,' or 'content' into the gap, as a sort of intermediary. Commonsense theories left the gap untouched, declaring our mind able to clear it by a self-transcending leap. Transcendentalist theories left it impossible to traverse by finite knowers, and brought an absolute in to perform the saltatory act. All the while, in the very bosom of the finite experience, every conjunction required

---

[1] Extract from an article entitled 'A World of Pure Experience,' in the *Journal of Philosophy, etc.*, September 29, 1904.

to make the relation intelligible is given in full. Either the knower and the known are:

(1) the self-same piece of experience taken twice over in different contexts; or they are

(2) two pieces of *actual* experience belonging to the same subject, with definite tracts of conjunctive transitional experience between them; or

(3) the known is a *possible* experience either of that subject or another, to which the said conjunctive transitions *would* lead, if sufficiently prolonged.

To discuss all the ways in which one experience may function as the knower of another, would be incompatible with the limits of this essay. I have treated of type 1, the kind of knowledge called perception, in an article in the *Journal of Philosophy*, for September 1, 1904, called 'Does consciousness exist?' This is the type of case in which the mind enjoys direct 'acquaintance' with a present object. In the other types the mind has 'knowledge-about' an object not immediately there. Type 3 can always formally and hypothetically be reduced to type 2, so that a brief description of that type will now put the present reader sufficiently at my point of view, and make him see what the actual meanings of the mysterious cognitive relation may be.

Suppose me to be sitting here in my library at Cambridge, at ten minutes' walk from 'Memorial Hall,' and to be thinking truly of the latter object. My mind may have before it only the name, or it may have a clear image, or it may have a very dim image of the hall, but such an intrinsic difference in the image makes no difference in its cognitive function. Certain *extrinsic* phenomena, special experiences of conjunction, are what impart to the image, be it what it may, its knowing office.

For instance, if you ask me what hall I mean by my image, and I can tell you nothing; or if I fail to point or lead you towards the Harvard Delta; or if, being led by you, I am uncertain whether the Hall I see be what I had in mind or not; you would rightly deny that I had 'meant' that particular hall at all, even tho my mental image might to some degree have

resembled it. The resemblance would count
in that case as coincidental merely, for all sorts
of things of a kind resemble one another in
this world without being held for that reason
to take cognizance of one another.

On the other hand, if I can lead you to the
hall, and tell you of its history and present
uses; if in its presence I feel my idea, however imperfect it may have been, to have led
hither and to be now *terminated;* if the associates of the image and of the felt hall run
parallel, so that each term of the one context
corresponds serially, as I walk, with an answer-
ing term of the other; why then my soul was
prophetic, and my idea must be, and by common consent would be, called cognizant of
reality. That percept was what I *meant,* for
into it my idea has passed by conjunctive experiences of sameness and fulfilled intention.
Nowhere is there jar, but every later moment
continues and corroborates an earlier one.

In this continuing and corroborating, taken
in no transcendental sense, but denoting definitely felt transitions, *lies all that the knowing*

of a percept by an idea can possibly contain or signify. Wherever such transitions are felt, the first experience *knows* the last one. Where they do not, or where even as possibles they can not, intervene, there can be no pretence of knowing. In this latter case the extremes will be connected, if connected at all, by inferior relations — bare likeness or succession, or by 'withness' alone. Knowledge of sensible realities thus comes to life inside the tissue of experience. It is *made;* and made by relations that unroll themselves in time. Whenever certain intermediaries are given, such that, as they develop towards their terminus, there is experience from point to point of one direction followed, and finally of one process fulfilled, the result is that *their starting-point thereby becomes a knower and their terminus an object meant or known.* That is all that knowing (in the simple case considered) can be known-as, that is the whole of its nature, put into experiential terms. Whenever such is the sequence of our experiences we may freely say that we had the terminal object 'in mind' from the outset, even altho *at* the outset nothing was there in us but a flat piece of substantive experience like any other, with no self-transcendency about it, and no mystery save the mystery of coming into existence and of being gradually followed by other pieces of substantive experience, with conjunctively transitional experiences between. That is what we *mean* here by the object's being 'in mind.' Of any deeper more real way of its being in mind we have no positive conception, and we have no right to discredit our actual experience by talking of such a way at all.

I know that many a reader will rebel at this. 'Mere intermediaries,' he will say, 'even tho they be feelings of continuously growing fulfilment, only *separate* the knower from the known, whereas what we have in knowledge is a kind of immediate touch of the one by the other, an "apprehension" in the etymological sense of the word, a leaping of the chasm as by lightning, an act by which two terms are smitten into one over the head of their distinctness. All these dead intermediaries of yours are out of each other, and outside of their termini still.'

But do not such dialectic difficulties remind us of the dog dropping his bone and snapping at its image in the water? If we knew any more real kind of union *aliunde,* we might be entitled to brand all our empirical unions as a sham. But unions by continuous transition are the only ones we know of, whether in this matter of a knowledge-about that terminates in an acquaintance, whether in personal identity, in logical prediction through the copula 'is,' or elsewhere. If anywhere there were more absolute unions, they could only reveal themselves to us by just such conjunctive results. These are what the unions are *worth,* these are all that *we can ever practically mean* by union, by continuity. Is it not time to repeat what Lotze said of substances, that to *act like* one is to *be* one? Should we not say here that to be experienced as continuous is to be really continuous, in a world where experience and reality come to the same thing? In a picture gallery a painted hook will serve to hang a painted chain by, a painted cable will hold a painted ship. In a world where both the terms and their distinctions are affairs of experience, conjunctions that are experienced must be at least as real as anything else. They will be 'absolutely' real conjunctions, if we have no transphenomenal absolute ready, to derealize the whole experienced world by, at a stroke.

So much for the essentials of the cognitive relation where the knowledge is conceptual in type, or forms knowledge 'about' an object. It consists in intermediary experiences (possible, if not actual) of continuously developing progress, and, finally, of fulfilment, when the sensible percept which is the object is reached. The percept here not only *verifies* the concept, proves its function of knowing that percept to be true, but the percept's existence as the terminus of the chain of intermediaries *creates* the function. Whatever terminates that chain was, because it now proves itself to be, what the concept 'had in mind.'

The towering importance for human life of this kind of knowing lies in the fact that an experience that knows another can figure as its *representative*, not in any quasi-miraculous 'epistemological' sense, but in the definite practical sense of being its *substitute* in various operations, sometimes physical and sometimes mental, which lead us to its associates and results. By experimenting on our ideas of reality, we may save ourselves the trouble of experimenting on the real experiences which they severally mean. The ideas form related systems, corresponding point for point to the systems which the realities form; and by letting an ideal term call up its associates systematically, we may be led to a terminus which the corresponding real term would have led to in case we had operated on the real world. And this brings us to the general question of substitution.

What, exactly, in a system of experiences, does the 'substitution' of one of them for another mean?

According to my view, experience as a whole is a process in time, whereby innumerable particular terms lapse and are superseded by others that follow upon them by transitions which, whether disjunctive or conjunctive in content, are themselves experiences, and must in general be accounted at least as real as the terms which they relate. What the nature of the event called 'superseding' signifies, depends altogether on the kind of transition that obtains. Some experiences simply abolish their predecessors without continuing them in any way. Others are felt to increase or to enlarge their meaning, to carry out their purpose, or to bring us nearer to their goal. They 'represent' them, and may fulfil their function better than they fulfilled it themselves. But to 'fulfil a function' in a world of pure experience can be conceived and defined in only one possible way. In such a world transitions and arrivals (or terminations) are the only events that happen, tho they happen by so many sorts of path. The only function that one experience can perform is to lead into another experience; and the only fulfilment we can speak of is the reaching of a certain experienced end. When one experience leads to (or can lead to) the same end as another, they agree in function. But the whole system of experiences as they are immediately given presents itself as a quasi-chaos through which one can pass out of an initial term in many directions and yet end in the same terminus, moving from next to next by a great many possible paths.

Either one of these paths might be a functional substitute for another, and to follow one rather than another might on occasion be an advantageous thing to do. As a matter of fact, and in a general way, the paths that run through conceptual experiences, that is, through 'thoughts' or 'ideas' that 'know' the things in which they terminate, are highly advantageous paths to follow. Not only do they yield inconceivably rapid transitions; but, owing to the 'universal' character [1] which

---

[1] Of which all that need be said in this essay is that it also can be conceived as functional, and defined in terms of transitions, or of the possibility of such.

they frequently possess, and to their capacity
for association with one another in great systems, they outstrip the tardy consecutions of
the things themselves, and sweep us on towards
our ultimate termini in a far more labor-saving
way than the following of trains of sensible
perception ever could. Wonderful are the new
cuts and the short-circuits the thought-paths
make. Most thought-paths, it is true, are substitutes for nothing actual; they end outside the
real world altogether, in wayward fancies, uto-
pias, fictions or mistakes. But where they do
re-enter reality and terminate therein, we substitute them always; and with these substitutes
we pass the greater number of our hours.[1]

[1] This is why I called our experiences, taken all together,
a quasi-chaos. There is vastly more discontinuity in the sum
total of experiences than we commonly suppose. The objective nucleus of every man's experience, his own body, is, it is
true, a continuous percept; and equally continuous as a percept (though we may be inattentive to it) is the material environment of that body, changing by gradual transition when
the body moves. But the distant parts of the physical world
are at all times absent from us, and form conceptual objects
merely, into the perceptual reality of which our life inserts
itself at points discrete and relatively rare. Round their several objective nuclei, partly shared and common partly dis-

Whosoever feels his experience to be something substitutional even while he has it, may be said to have an experience that reaches beyond itself. From inside of its own entity it says 'more,' and postulates reality existing elsewhere. For the transcendentalist, who holds knowing to consist in a *salto mortale* across an 'epistemological chasm,' such an idea presents no difficulty; but it seems at first sight as if it might be inconsistent with an empiricism like our own. Have we not explained that conceptual knowledge is made such wholly by the existence of things that fall outside of the knowing experience itself — by intermediary experiences and by a terminus that fulfils?

crete, of the real physical world, innumerable thinkers, pursuing their several lines of physically true cogitation, trace paths that intersect one another only at discontinuous perceptual points, and the rest of the time are quite incongruent; and around all the nuclei of shared 'reality' floats the vast cloud of experiences that are wholly subjective, that are non-substitutional, that find not even an eventual ending for themselves in the perceptual world — the mere day-dreams and joys and sufferings and wishes of the individual minds. These exist *with* one another, indeed, and with the objective nuclei, but out of them it is probable that to all eternity no inter-related system of any kind will ever be made.

Can the knowledge be there before these elements that constitute its being have come? And, if knowledge be not there, how can objective reference occur?

The key to this difficulty lies in the distinction between knowing as verified and completed, and the same knowing as in transit and on its way. To recur to the Memorial Hall example lately used, it is only when our idea of the Hall has actually terminated in the percept that we know 'for certain' that from the beginning it was truly cognitive of *that*. Until established by the end of the process, its quality of knowing that, or indeed of knowing anything, could still be doubted; and yet the knowing really was there, as the result now shows. We were *virtual* knowers of the Hall long before we were certified to have been its actual knowers, by the percept's retroactive validating power. Just so we are 'mortal' all the time, by reason of the virtuality of the inevitable event which will make us so when it shall have come.

Now the immensely greater part of all our

knowing never gets beyond this virtual stage. It never is completed or nailed down. I speak not merely of our ideas of imperceptibles like ether-waves or dissociated 'ions,' or of 'ejects' like the contents of our neighbors' minds; I speak also of ideas which we might verify if we would take the trouble, but which we hold for true altho unterminated perceptually, because nothing says 'no' to us, and there is no contradicting truth in sight. *To continue thinking unchallenged is, ninety-nine times out of a hundred, our practical substitute for knowing in the completed sense.* As each experience runs by cognitive transition into the next one, and we nowhere feel a collision with what we elsewhere count as truth or fact, we commit ourselves to the current as if the port were sure. We live, as it were, upon the front edge of an advancing wave-crest, and our sense of a determinate direction in falling forward is all we cover of the future of our path. It is as if a differential quotient should be conscious and treat itself as an adequate substitute for a traced-out curve. Our experience, *inter alia*, is of variations of rate and of direction, and lives in these transitions more than in the journey's end. The experiences of tendency are sufficient to act upon — what more could we have *done* at those moments even if the later verification comes complete?

This is what, as a radical empiricist, I say to the charge that the objective reference which is so flagrant a character of our experiences involves a chasm and a mortal leap. A positively conjunctive transition involves neither chasm nor leap. Being the very original of what we mean by continuity, it makes a continuum wherever it appears. Objective reference is an incident of the fact that so much of our experience comes as an insufficient and consists of process and transition. Our fields of experience have no more definite boundaries than have our fields of view. Both are fringed forever by a *more* that continuously develops, and that continuously supersedes them as life proceeds. The relations, generally speaking, are as real here as the terms are, and the only complaint of the transcendentalist's with which I could at all sympathize would be his charge that, by first making knowledge to consist in external relations as I have done, and by then confessing that nine-tenths of the time these are not actually but only virtually there, I have knocked the solid bottom out of the whole business, and palmed off a substitute of knowledge for the genuine thing. Only the admission, such a critic might say, that our ideas are self-transcendent and 'true' already; in advance of the experiences that are to terminate them, can bring solidity back to knowledge in a world like this, in which transitions and terminations are only by exception fulfilled.

This seems to me an excellent place for applying the pragmatic method. What would the self-transcendency affirmed to exist in advance of all experiential mediation or termination, be *known-as?* What would it practically result in for *us*, were it true?

It could only result in our orientation, in the turning of our expectations and practical tendencies into the right path; and the right path here, so long as we and the object are not yet face to face (or can never get face to face, as in the case of ejects), would be the path that led us into the object's nearest neighborhood. Where direct acquaintance is lacking, 'knowledge about' is the next best thing, and an acquaintance with what actually lies about the object, and is most closely related to it, puts such knowledge within our grasp. Ether-waves and your anger, for example, are things in which my thoughts will never *perceptually* terminate, but my concepts of them lead me to their very brink, to the chromatic fringes and to the hurtful words and deeds which are their really next effects.

Even if our ideas did in themselves possess the postulated self-transcendency, it would still remain true that their putting us into possession of such effects *would be the sole cash-value of the self-transcendency for us.* And this cash-value, it is needless to say, is *verbatim et literatim* what our empiricist account pays in. On pragmatist principles therefore, a dispute over self-transcendency is a pure logomachy. Call our concepts of ejective things self-transcendent or the reverse, it makes no difference, so long as we don't differ about the nature of that exalted virtue's fruits — fruits for us, of course, humanistic fruits.

The transcendentalist believes his ideas to be self-transcendent only because he finds that in fact they do bear fruits. Why need he quarrel with an account of knowledge that insists on naming this effect? Why not treat the working of the idea from next to next as the essence of its self-transcendency? Why insist that knowing is a static relation out of time when it practically seems so much a function of our active life? For a thing to be valid, says Lotze, is the same as to make itself valid. When the whole universe seems only to be making itself valid and to be still incomplete (else why its ceaseless changing?) why, of all things, should knowing be exempt? Why should it not be making itself valid like everything else? That some parts of it may be already valid or verified beyond dispute, the empirical philosopher, of course, like any one else, may always hope.

V

THE ESSENCE OF HUMANISM [1]

HUMANISM is a ferment that has 'come to stay.' It is not a single hypothesis or theorem, and it dwells on no new facts. It is rather a slow shifting in the philosophic perspective, making things appear as from a new centre of interest or point of sight. Some writers are strongly conscious of the shifting, others half unconscious, even though their own vision may have undergone much change. The result is no small confusion in debate, the half-conscious humanists often taking part against the radical ones, as if they wished to count upon the other side. [2]

If humanism really be the name for such

[1] Reprinted from the *Journal of Philosophy, Psychology and Scientific Methods*, vol. ii, No. 5, March 2, 1905.

[2] Professor Baldwin, for example. His address 'Selective Thinking' (*Psychological Review*, January, 1898, reprinted in his volume, 'Development and Evolution') seems to me an unusually well written pragmatic manifesto. Nevertheless in 'The Limits of Pragmatism' (*ibid.*, January, 1904), he (much less clearly) joins in the attack.

a shifting of perspective, it is obvious that the whole scene of the philosophic stage will change in some degree if humanism prevails. The emphasis of things, their foreground and background distribution, their sizes and values, will not keep just the same.[1] If such pervasive consequences be involved in humanism, it is clear that no pains which philosophers may take, first in defining it, and then in furthering, checking, or steering its progress, will be thrown away.

It suffers badly at present from incomplete definition. Its most systematic advocates, Schiller and Dewey, have published fragmentary programmes only; and its bearing on many

[1] The ethical changes, it seems to me, are beautifully made evident in Professor Dewey's series of articles, which will never get the attention they deserve till they are printed in a book. I mean: 'The Significance of Emotions,' *Psychological Review*, vol. ii, 13; 'The Reflex Arc Concept in Psychology,' *ibid.*, iii, 357; 'Psychology and Social Practice,' *ibid.*, vii, 105; 'Interpretation of Savage Mind,' *ibid.*, ix, 217; 'Green's Theory of the Moral Motive,' *Philosophical Review*, vol. i, 593; 'Self-realization as the Moral Ideal,' *ibid.*, ii, 652; 'The Psychology of Effort,' *ibid.*, vi, 43; 'The Evolutionary Method as Applied to Morality,' *ibid.*, xi, 107, 353; 'Evolution and Ethics,' *Monist*, vol. viii, 321; to mention only a few.

vital philosophic problems has not been traced except by adversaries who, scenting heresies in advance, have showered blows on doctrines — subjectivism and scepticism, for example — that no good humanist finds it necessary to entertain. By their still greater reticences, the anti-humanists have, in turn, perplexed the humanists. Much of the controversy has involved the word 'truth.' It is always good in debate to know your adversary's point of view authentically. But the critics of humanism never define exactly what the word 'truth' signifies when they use it themselves. The humanists have to guess at their view; and the result has doubtless been much beating of the air. Add to all this, great individual differences in both camps, and it becomes clear that nothing is so urgently needed, at the stage which things have reached at present, as a sharper definition by each side of its central point of view.

Whoever will contribute any touch of sharpness will help us to make sure of what's what and who is who. Any one can contribute such a definition, and, without it, no one knows exactly where he stands. If I offer my own provisional definition of humanism now and here, others may improve it, some adversary may be led to define his own creed more sharply by the contrast, and a certain quickening of the crystallization of general opinion may result.

I

The essential service of humanism, as I conceive the situation, is to have seen that *tho one part of our experience may lean upon another part to make it what it is in any one of several aspects in which it may be considered, experience as a whole is self-containing and leans on nothing.* Since this formula also expresses the main contention of transcendental idealism, it needs abundant explication to make it unambiguous. It seems, at first sight, to confine itself to denying theism and pantheism. But, in fact, it need not deny either; everything would depend on the exegesis; and if the formula ever became canonical, it would certainly develop both right-wing and left-wing interpreters. I myself read humanism theistically and pluralistically. If there be a God, he is no absolute all-experiencer, but simply the experiencer of widest actual conscious span. Read thus, humanism is for me a religion susceptible of reasoned defence, tho I am well aware how many minds there are to whom it can appeal religiously only when it has been monistically translated. Ethically the pluralistic form of it takes for me a stronger hold on reality than any other philosophy I know of — it being essentially a *social* philosophy, a philosophy of '*co*,' in which conjunctions do the work. But my primary reason for advocating it is its matchless intellectual economy. It gets rid, not only of the standing 'problems' that monism engenders ('problem of evil,' 'problem of freedom,' and the like), but of other metaphysical mysteries and paradoxes as well.

It gets rid, for example, of the whole agnostic controversy, by refusing to entertain the hypothesis of trans-empirical reality at all. It gets rid of any need for an absolute of the bradleyan type (avowedly sterile for intellectual purposes) by insisting that the conjunctive relations found within experience are faultlessly real. It gets rid of the need of an absolute of the roycean type (similarly sterile) by its pragmatic treatment of the problem of knowledge. As the views of knowledge, reality and truth imputed to humanism have been those so far most fiercely attacked, it is in regard to these ideas that a sharpening of focus seems most urgently required. I proceed therefore to bring the views which *I* impute to humanism in these respects into focus as briefly as I can.

II

If the central humanistic thesis, printed above in italics, be accepted, it will follow that, if there be any such thing at all as knowing, the knower and the object known must both be portions of experience. One part of experience must, therefore, either

(1) Know another part of experience — in other words, parts must, as Professor Wood-

bridge says,[1] represent *one another* instead of representing realities outside of 'consciousness' — this case is that of conceptual knowledge; or else

(2) They must simply exist as so many ultimate *thats* or facts of being, in the first instance; and then, as a secondary complication, and without doubling up its entitative singleness, any one and the same *that* in experience must figure alternately as a thing known and as a knowledge of the thing, by reason of two divergent kinds of context into which, in the general course of experience, it gets woven.[2]

This second case is that of sense-perception. There is a stage of thought that goes beyond common sense, and of it I shall say more presently; but the common-sense stage is a perfectly definite halting-place of thought, primarily for purposes of action; and, so long

[1] In *Science*, November 4, 1904, p. 599.

[2] This statement is probably excessively obscure to any one who has not read my two articles 'Does Consciousness Exist?' and 'A World of Pure Experience' in the *Journal of Philosophy*, vol. i, 1904.

as we remain on the common-sense stage of thought, object and subject *fuse* in the fact of 'presentation' or sense-perception — the pen and hand which I now *see* writing, for example, *are* the physical realities which those words designate. In this case there is no self-transcendency implied in the knowing. Humanism, here, is only a more comminuted *identitätsphilosophie*.

In case (1), on the contrary, the representative experience *does transcend itself* in knowing the other experience that is its object. No one can talk of the knowledge of the one by the other without seeing them as numerically distinct entities, of which the one lies beyond the other and away from it, along some direction and with some interval, that can be definitely named. But, if the talker be a humanist, he must also see this distance-interval concretely and pragmatically, and confess it to consist of other intervening experiences — of possible ones, at all events, if not of actual. To call my present idea of my dog, for example, cognitive of the real dog means that, as the actual tissue of experience is constituted, the idea is capable of leading into a chain of other experiences on my part that go from next to next and terminate at last in vivid sense-perceptions of a jumping, barking, hairy body. Those *are* the real dog, the dog's full presence, for my common sense. If the supposed talker is a profound philosopher, altho they may not *be* the real dog for him, they *mean* the real dog, are practical substitutes for the real dog, as the representation was a practical substitute for them, that real dog being a lot of atoms, say, or of mindstuff, that lie *where* the sense-perceptions lie in his experience as well as in my own.

III

The philosopher here stands for the stage of thought that goes beyond the stage of common sense; and the difference is simply that he 'interpolates' and 'extrapolates,' where common sense does not. For common sense, two men see the same identical real dog. Philosophy, noting actual differences in their perceptions, points out the duality of these latter, and interpolates something between them as a more real terminus — first, organs, viscera, etc.; next, cells; then, ultimate atoms; lastly, mind-stuff perhaps. The original sense-termini of the two men, instead of coalescing with each other and with the real dog-object, as at first supposed, are thus held by philosophers to be separated by invisible realities with which, at most, they are conterminous.

Abolish, now, one of the percipients, and the interpolation changes into 'extrapolation.' The sense-terminus of the remaining percipient is regarded by the philosopher as not quite reaching reality. He has only carried the procession of experiences, the philosopher thinks, to a definite, because practical, halting-place somewhere on the way towards an absolute truth that lies beyond.

The humanist sees all the time, however, that there is no absolute transcendency even about the more absolute realities thus conjectured or believed in. The viscera and cells are only possible percepts following upon that of the outer body. The atoms again, tho we may never attain to human means of perceiving them, are still defined perceptually. The mind-stuff itself is conceived as a kind of experience; and it is possible to frame the hypothesis (such hypotheses can by no logic be excluded from philosophy) of two knowers of a piece of mind-stuff and the mind-stuff itself becoming 'confluent' at the moment at which our imperfect knowing might pass into knowing of a completed type. Even so do you and I habitually conceive our two perceptions and the real dog as confluent, tho only provisionally, and for the common-sense stage of thought. If my pen be inwardly made of mind-stuff, there is no confluence *now* between that mind-stuff and my visual perception of the pen. But conceivably there might come to be such confluence; for, in the case of my *hand*, the visual sensations and the inward feelings of the hand, its mind-stuff, so to speak, are even now as confluent as any two things can be.

There is, thus, no breach in humanistic

131

epistemology. Whether knowledge be taken as ideally perfected, or only as true enough to pass muster for practice, it is hung on one continuous scheme. Reality, howsoever remote, is always defined as a terminus within the general possibilities of experience; and what knows it is defined as an experience *that 'represents' it, in the sense of being substitutable for it in our thinking* because it leads to the same associates, *or in the sense of 'pointing to it' through a chain of other experiences that either intervene or may intervene.*

Absolute reality here bears the same relation to sensation as sensation bears to conception or imagination. Both are provisional or final termini, sensation being only the terminus at which the practical man habitually stops, while the philosopher projects a 'beyond,' in the shape of more absolute reality. These termini, for the practical and the philosophical stages of thought respectively, are self-supporting. They are not 'true' of anything else, they simply *are*, are *real*. They 'lean on nothing,' as my italicized formula said. Rather does the whole fabric of experience lean on them, just as the whole fabric of the solar system, including many relative positions, leans, for its absolute position in space, on any one of its constituent stars. Here, again, one gets a new *Identitäts-philosophie* in pluralistic form.

IV

If I have succeeded in making this at all clear (tho I fear that brevity and abstractness between them may have made me fail), the reader will see that the 'truth' of our mental operations must always be an intra-experiential affair. A conception is reckoned true by common sense when it can be made to lead to a sensation. The sensation, which for common sense is not so much 'true' as 'real,' is held to be *provisionally* true by the philosopher just in so far as it *covers* (abuts at, or occupies the place of) a still more absolutely real experience, in the possibility of which, to some remoter experient, the philosopher finds reason to believe.

Meanwhile what actually *does* count for

true to any individual trower, whether he be philosopher or common man, is always a result of his *apperceptions.* If a novel experience, conceptual or sensible, contradict too emphatically our pre-existent system of beliefs, in ninety-nine cases out of a hundred it is treated as false. Only when the older and the newer experiences are congruous enough to mutually apperceive and modify each other, does what we treat as an advance in truth result. In no case, however, need truth consist in a relation between our experiences and something archetypal or trans-experiential. Should we ever reach absolutely terminal experiences, experiences in which we all agreed, which were superseded by no revised continuations, these would not be *true*, they would be *real*, they would simply *be*, and be indeed the angles, corners, and linchpins of all reality, on which the truth of everything else would be stayed. Only such *other* things as led to these by satisfactory conjunctions would be 'true.' Satisfactory connection of some sort with such termini is all that the word 'truth' means. On the common-sense stage of thought sense-presentations serve as such termini. Our ideas and concepts and scientific theories pass for true only so far as they harmoniously lead back to the world of sense.

I hope that many humanists will endorse this attempt of mine to trace the more essential features of that way of viewing things. I feel almost certain that Messrs. Dewey and Schiller will do so. If the attackers will also take some slight account of it, it may be that discussion will be a little less wide of the mark than it has hitherto been.

VI

A WORD MORE ABOUT TRUTH

MY failure in making converts to my conception of truth seems, if I may judge by what I hear in conversation, almost complete. An ordinary philosopher would feel disheartened, and a common choleric sinner would curse God and die, after such a reception. But instead of taking counsel of despair, I make bold to vary my statements, in the faint hope that repeated droppings may wear upon the stone, and that my formulas may seem less obscure if surrounded by something more of a 'mass' whereby to apperceive them.

For fear of compromising other pragmatists, whoe'er they be, I will speak of the conception which I am trying to make intelligible, as my own conception. I first published it in the year 1885, in the first article reprinted in the present book. Essential theses of this article were independently supported in 1893 and 1895 by

[1] Reprint from the *Journal of Philosophy*, July 18, 1907.

Professor D. S. Miller [1] and were repeated by
me in a presidential address on 'The knowing of things together' [2] in 1895. Professor
Strong, in an article in the *Journal of Philosophy, etc.,* [3] entitled 'A naturalistic theory of
the reference of thought to reality,' called our
account 'the James-Miller theory of cognition,'
and, as I understood him, gave it his adhesion.
Yet, such is the difficulty of writing clearly in
these penetralia of philosophy, that each of these
revered colleagues informs me privately that
the account of truth I now give — which to me
is but that earlier statement more completely
set forth — is to him inadequate, and seems to
leave the gist of real cognition out. If such
near friends disagree, what can I hope from
remoter ones, and what from unfriendly critics?

Yet I feel so sure that the fault must lie in
my lame forms of statement and not in my
doctrine, that I am fain to try once more to
express myself.

[1] *Philosophical Review,* vol. ii, p. 408, and *Psychological
Review,* vol. ii, p. 533.
[2] The relevant parts of which are printed above, p. 43.
[3] Vol. i, p. 253.

I

Are there not some general distinctions which it may help us to agree about in advance? Professor Strong distinguishes between what he calls 'saltatory' and what he calls 'ambulatory' relations. 'Difference,' for example, is saltatory, jumping as it were immediately from one term to another, but 'distance' in time or space is made out of intervening parts of experience through which we ambulate in succession. Years ago, when T. H. Green's ideas were most influential, I was much troubled by his criticisms of english sensationalism. One of his disciples in particular would always say to me, 'Yes! *terms* may indeed be possibly sensational in origin; but *relations*, what are they but pure acts of the intellect coming upon the sensations from above, and of a higher nature?' I well remember the sudden relief it gave me to perceive one day that *space*-relations at any rate were homogeneous with the terms between which they mediated. The terms were spaces, and the relations were

138

other intervening spaces.[1] For the Greenites space-relations had been saltatory, for me they became thenceforward ambulatory.

Now the most general way of contrasting my view of knowledge with the popular view (which is also the view of most epistemologists) is to call my view ambulatory, and the other view saltatory; and the most general way of characterizing the two views is by saying that my view describes knowing as it exists concretely, while the other view only describes its results abstractly taken.

I fear that most of my recalcitrant readers fail to recognize that what is ambulatory in the concrete may be taken so abstractly as to appear saltatory. Distance, for example, is made abstract by emptying out whatever is particular in the concrete intervals — it is reduced thus to a sole 'difference,' a difference of 'place,' which is a logical or saltatory distinction, a so-called 'pure relation.'

The same is true of the relation called 'knowing,' which may connect an idea with a reality.

[1] See my *Principles of Psychology*, vol. ii, pp. 148–153.

My own account of this relation is ambulatory through and through. I say that we know an object by means of an idea, whenever we ambulate towards the object under the impulse which the idea communicates. If we believe in so-called 'sensible' realities, the idea may not only send us towards its object, but may put the latter into our very hand, make it our immediate sensation. But, if, as most reflective people opine, sensible realities are not 'real' realities, but only their appearances, our idea brings us at least so far, puts us in touch with reality's most authentic appearances and substitutes. In any case our idea brings us into the object's neighborhood, practical or ideal, gets us into commerce with it, helps us towards its closer acquaintance, enables us to foresee it, class it, compare it, deduce it, — in short, to deal with it as we could not were the idea not in our possession.

The idea is thus, when functionally considered, an instrument for enabling us the better to *have to do* with the object and to act about it. But it and the object are both of them bits of the general sheet and tissue of reality at large; and when we say that the idea leads us towards the object, that only means that it carries us forward through intervening tracts of that reality into the object's closer neighborhood, into the midst of its associates at least, be these its physical neighbors, or be they its logical congeners only. Thus carried into closer quarters, we are in an improved situation as regards acquaintance and conduct; and we say that through the idea we now *know* the object better or more truly.

My thesis is that the knowing here is *made* by the ambulation through the intervening experiences. If the idea led us nowhere, or *from* that object instead of towards it, could we talk at all of its having any cognitive quality? Surely not, for it is only when taken in conjunction with the intermediate experiences that it gets related to *that particular object* rather than to any other part of nature. Those intermediaries determine what particular knowing function it exerts. The terminus they guide us to tells us what object it 'means,' the results they enrich us with 'verify' or 'refute' it. Intervening experiences are thus as indispensable foundations for a concrete relation of cognition as intervening space is for a relation of distance. Cognition, whenever we take it concretely, means determinate 'ambulation,' through intermediaries, from a *terminus a quo* to, or towards, a *terminus ad quem*. As the intermediaries are other than the termini, and connected with them by the usual associative bonds (be these 'external' or be they logical, *i. e.*, classificatory, in character), there would appear to be nothing especially unique about the processes of knowing. They fall wholly within experience; and we need use, in describing them, no other categories than those which we employ in describing other natural processes.

But there exist no processes which we cannot also consider abstractly, eviscerating them down to their essential skeletons or outlines; and when we have treated the processes of knowing thus, we are easily led to regard them as something altogether unparalleled in nature. For we first empty idea, object and intermediaries of all their particularities, in order to retain only a general scheme, and then we consider the latter only in its function of giving a result, and not in its character of being a process. In this treatment the intermediaries shrivel into the form of a mere space of separation, while the idea and object retain only the logical distinctness of being the end-terms that are separated. In other words, the intermediaries which in their concrete particularity form a bridge, evaporate ideally into an empty interval to cross, and then, the relation of the end-terms having become saltatory, the whole hocus-pocus of *erkenntnisstheorie* begins, and goes on unrestrained by further concrete considerations. The idea, in 'meaning' an object separated by an 'epistemological chasm' from itself, now executes what Professor Ladd calls a '*salto mortale*'; in knowing the object's nature, it now 'transcends' its own. The object in turn becomes 'present' where it is really absent, etc.; until a scheme remains upon our hands, the sublime paradoxes of which some of us think that nothing short of an 'absolute' can explain.

The relation between idea and object, thus made abstract and saltatory, is thenceforward opposed, as being more essential and previous, to its own ambulatory self, and the more concrete description is branded as either false or insufficient. The bridge of intermediaries, actual or possible, which in every real case is what carries and defines the knowing, gets treated as an episodic complication which need not even potentially be there. I believe that this vulgar fallacy of opposing abstractions to the concretes from which they are abstracted, is the main reason why my account of knowing is deemed so unsatisfactory, and I will therefore say a word more on that general point.

Any vehicle of conjunction, if *all* its particularities are abstracted from it, will leave us with nothing on our hands but the original disjunction which it bridged over. But to escape treating the resultant self-contradiction as an achievement of dialectical profundity, all we need is to restore some part, no matter how

144

small, of what we have taken away. In the case of the epistemological chasm the first reasonable step is to remember that the chasm was filled with *some* empirical material, whether ideational or sensational, which performed *some* bridging function and saved us from the mortal leap. Restoring thus the indispensable modicum of reality to the matter of our discussion, we find our abstract treatment genuinely useful. We escape entanglement with special cases without at the same time falling into gratuitous paradoxes. We can now describe the general features of cognition, tell what on the whole it *does for us*, in a universal way.

We must remember that this whole inquiry into knowing grows up on a reflective level. In any real moment of knowing, what we are thinking of is our object, not the way in which we ourselves are momentarily knowing it. We at this moment, as it happens, have knowing itself for our object; but I think that the reader will agree that his present knowing of that object is included only abstractly, and by anticipation, in the results he may reach. What he concretely has before his mind, as he reasons, is some supposed objective instance of knowing, as he conceives it to go on in some other person, or recalls it from his own past. As such, he, the critic, sees it to contain both an idea and an object, and processes by which the knower is guided from the one towards the other. He sees that the idea is remote from the object, and that, whether through intermediaries or not, it genuinely *has to do* with it. He sees that it thus works beyond its immediate being, and lays hold of a remote reality; it jumps across, transcends itself. It does all this by extraneous aid, to be sure, but when the aid has come, it *has* done it and the result is secure. Why not talk of results by themselves, then, without considering means? Why not treat the idea as simply grasping or intuiting the reality, of its having the faculty anyhow, of shooting over nature behind the scenes and knowing things immediately and directly? Why need we always lug in the bridging? — it only retards our discourse to do so.

Such abstract talk about cognition's results is surely convenient; and it is surely as legitimate as it is convenient, *so long as we do not forget or positively deny, what it ignores.* We may on occasion say that our idea meant *always* that particular object, that it led us there because it was *of* it intrinsically and essentially. We may insist that its verification follows upon that original cognitive virtue in it — and all the rest — and we shall do no harm so long as we know that these are only short cuts in our thinking. They are positively true accounts of fact *as far as they go*, only they leave vast tracts of fact out of the account, tracts of fact that have to be reinstated to make the accounts literally true of any real case. But if, not merely passively ignoring the intermediaries, you actively deny them [1] to be even potential requisites for the results you are so struck by, your epistemology goes to irremediable smash. You are as far

[1] This is the fallacy which I have called 'vicious intellectualism' in my book *A Pluralistic Universe*, Longmans, Green & Co., 1909.

off the track as an historian would be, if, lost in admiration of Napoleon's personal power, he were to ignore his marshals and his armies, and were to accuse you of error in describing his conquests as effected by their means. Of such abstractness and one-sidedness I accuse most of the critics of my own account.

In the second lecture of the book *Pragmatism*, I used the illustration of a squirrel scrambling round a tree-trunk to keep out of sight of a pursuing man: both go round the tree, but does the man go round the squirrel? It all depends, I said, on what you mean by 'going round.' In one sense of the word the man 'goes round,' in another sense he does not. I settled the dispute by pragmatically distinguishing the senses. But I told how some disputants had called my distinction a shuffling evasion and taken their stand on what they called 'plain honest English going-round.'

In such a simple case few people would object to letting the term in dispute be translated into its concreter equivalents. But in the case of a complex function like our knowing

148

they act differently. I give full concrete particular value for the ideas of knowing in every case I can think of, yet my critics insist that 'plain honest English knowing' is left out of my account. They write as if the minus were on my side and the plus on theirs.

The essence of the matter for me is that altho knowing can be both abstractly and concretely described, and altho the abstract descriptions are often useful enough, yet they are all sucked up and absorbed without residuum into the concreter ones, and contain nothing of any essentially other or higher nature, which the concrete descriptions can be justly accused of leaving behind. Knowing is just a natural process like any other. There is no ambulatory process whatsoever, the results of which we may not describe, if we prefer to, in saltatory terms, or represent in static formulation. Suppose, *e. g.*, that we say a man is 'prudent.' Concretely, that means that he takes out insurance, hedges in betting, looks before he leaps. Do such acts *constitute* the prudence? *are* they the man quâ prudent?

Or is the prudence something by itself and independent of them? As a constant habit in him, a permanent tone of character, it is convenient to call him prudent in abstraction from any one of his acts, prudent in general and without specification, and to say the acts follow from the pre-existing prudence. There are peculiarities in his psycho-physical system that make him act prudently; and there are tendencies to association in our thoughts that prompt some of them to make for truth and others for error. But would the man be prudent in the absence of each and all of the acts? Or would the thoughts be true if they had no associative or impulsive tendencies? Surely we have no right to oppose static essences in this way to the moving processes in which they live embedded.

My bedroom is above my library. Does the 'aboveness' here mean aught that is different from the concrete spaces which have to be moved-through in getting from the one to the other? It means, you may say, a pure topographic relation, a sort of architect's plan among the eternal essences. But that is not the full aboveness, it is only an abbreviated substitute that on occasion may lead my mind towards truer, *i. e.*, fuller, dealings with the real aboveness. It is not an aboveness *ante rem*, it is a *post rem* extract from the aboveness *in rebus*. We may indeed talk, for certain conveniences, as if the abstract scheme preceded, we may say 'I must go up stairs because of the essential aboveness,' just as we may say that the man 'does prudent acts because of his ingrained prudence,' or that our ideas 'lead us truly because of their intrinsic truth.' But this should not debar us on other occasions from using completer forms of description. A concrete matter of fact always remains identical under any form of description, as when we say of a line, now that it runs from left to right, and now that it runs from right to left. These are but names of one and the same fact, one more expedient to use at one time, one at another. The *full* facts of cognition, whatever be the way in which we talk about them, even when

151

we talk most abstractly, stand inalterably given in the actualities and possibilities of the experience-continuum.[1] But my critics treat my own more concrete talk as if *it* were the kind that sinned by its inadequacy, and as if the full continuum left something out.

A favorite way of opposing the more abstract to the more concrete account is to accuse those who favor the latter of 'confounding psychology with logic.' Our critics say that when we are asked what truth *means*, we reply by telling only how it is *arrived-at*. But since a meaning is a logical relation, static, independent of time, how can it possibly be identified, they say, with any concrete man's experience, perishing as this does at the instant of its production? This, indeed, sounds profound, but I challenge the profundity. I defy any one to show any difference between logic

[1] The ultimate object or terminus of a cognitive process may in certain instances lie beyond the direct experience of the particular cognizer, but it, of course, must exist as part of the total universe of experience whose constitution, with cognition in it, the critic is discussing.

and psychology here. The logical relation stands to the psychological relation between idea and object only as saltatory abstractness stands to ambulatory concreteness. Both relations need a psychological vehicle; and the 'logical' one is simply the 'psychological' one disemboweled of its fulness, and reduced to a bare abstractional scheme.

A while ago a prisoner, on being released, tried to assassinate the judge who had sentenced him. He had apparently succeeded in conceiving the judge timelessly, had reduced him to a bare logical meaning, that of being his 'enemy and persecutor,' by stripping off all the concrete conditions (as jury's verdict, official obligation, absence of personal spite, possibly sympathy) that gave its full psychological character to the sentence as a particular man's act in time. Truly the sentence *was* inimical to the culprit; but which idea of it is the truer one, that bare logical definition of it, or its full psychological specification? The anti-pragmatists ought in consistency to stand up for the criminal's view of the case, treat the judge as the latter's logical enemy, and bar out the other conditions as so much inessential psychological stuff.

II

A still further obstacle, I suspect, stands in the way of my account's acceptance. Like Dewey and like Schiller, I have had to say that the truth of an idea is determined by its satisfactoriness. But satisfactoriness is a subjective term, just as idea is; and truth is generally regarded as 'objective.' Readers who admit that satisfactoriness is our only *mark* of truth, the only sign that we possess the precious article, will still say that the objective relation between idea and object which the word 'truth' points to is left out of my account altogether. I fear also that the association of my poor name with the 'will to believe' (which 'will,' it seems to me, ought to play no part in this discussion) works against my credit in some quarters. I fornicate with that unclean thing, my adversaries may think, whereas your genuine truth-lover must discourse in huxleyan heroics, and feel as if truth, to be real truth, ought to bring eventual messages of death to all our satisfactions. Such divergences certainly prove the complexity of the area of our discussion; but to my mind they also are based on misunderstandings, which (tho with but little hope of success) I will try to diminish by a further word of explanation.

First, then, I will ask my objectors to define exactly what *sort* of thing it is they have in mind when they speak of a truth that shall be absolute, complete and objective; and then I will defy them to show me any conceivable standing-room for such a kind of truth outside the terms of my own description. It will fall, as I contend, entirely within the field of my analysis.

To begin with, it must obtain between an idea and a reality that is the idea's object; and, as a predicate, it must apply to the idea and not to the object, for objective realities are not *true*, at least not in the universe of discourse to which we are now confining ourselves, for there they are taken as simply *being*, while the ideas are true *of* them. But we can suppose a series of ideas to be successively more and more true of the same object, and can ask what is the extreme approach to being absolutely true that the last idea might attain to.

The maximal conceivable truth in an idea would seem to be that it should lead to an actual merging of ourselves with the object, to an utter mutual confluence and identification. On the common-sense level of belief this is what is supposed really to take place in sense-perception. My idea of this pen verifies itself through my percept; and my percept is held to *be* the pen for the time being — percepts and physical realities being treated by common sense as identical. But the physiology of the senses has criticised common sense out of court, and the pen 'in itself' is now believed to lie beyond my momentary percept. Yet the notion once suggested, of what a completely consummated acquaintance with a reality might be like, remains over for our speculative purposes. *Total conflux of the mind with the reality* would be the absolute limit of truth, there could be no better or more satisfying knowledge than that.

Such total conflux, it is needless to say, is *already explicitly provided for, as a possibility, in my account of the matter.* If an idea should ever lead us not only *towards*, or *up to*, or *against*, a reality, but so close that we and the reality should *melt together*, it would be made absolutely true, according to me, by that performance.

In point of fact philosophers doubt that this ever occurs. What happens, they think, is only that we get nearer and nearer to realities, we approximate more and more to the all-satisfying limit; and the definition of actually, as distinguished from imaginably, complete and objective truth, can then only be that it belongs to the idea that will lead us as *close up against the object* as in the nature of our experience is possible, literally *next* to it, for instance.

Suppose, now, there were an idea that did this for a certain objective reality. Suppose that no further approach were possible, that nothing lay between, that the next step would carry us right *into* the reality; then that result, being the next thing to conflux, would make the idea true in the maximal degree that might be supposed practically attainable in the world which we inhabit.

Well, I need hardly explain that *that degree of truth is also provided for in my account of the matter*. And if satisfactions are the marks of truth's presence, we may add that any less true substitute for such a true idea would prove less satisfactory. Following its lead, we should probably find out that we did not quite touch the terminus. We should desiderate a closer approach, and not rest till we had found it.

I am, of course, postulating here a standing reality independent of the idea that knows it. I am also postulating that satisfactions grow *pari passu* with our approximation to such reality.[1] If my critics challenge this latter

---

[1] Say, if you prefer to, that *dis*satisfactions decrease *pari passu* with such approximation. The approximation may be of any kind assignable — approximation in time or in space, or approximation in kind, which in common speech means 'copying.'

assumption, I retort upon them with the for, mer. Our whole notion of a standing reality grows up in the form of an ideal limit to the series of successive termini to which our thoughts have led us and still are leading us. Each terminus proves provisional by leaving us unsatisfied. The truer idea is the one that pushes farther; so we are ever beckoned on by the ideal notion of an ultimate completely satisfactory terminus. I, for one, obey and accept that notion. I can conceive no other objective *content* to the notion of ideally per, fect truth than that of penetration into such a terminus, nor can I conceive that the notion would ever have grown up, or that true ideas would ever have been sorted out from false or idle ones, save for the greater sum of satis-factions, intellectual or practical, which the truer ones brought with them. Can we im-agine a man absolutely satisfied with an idea and with all its relations to his other ideas and to his sensible experiences, who should yet *not* take its content as a true account of reality? The *matter* of the true is thus absolutely identical with the matter of the satisfactory. You may put either word first in your ways of talking; but leave out that whole notion of *satisfactory working* or *leading* (which is the essence of my pragmatistic account) and call truth a static logical relation, independent even of *possible* leadings or satisfactions, and it seems to me you cut all ground from under you.

I fear that I am still very obscure. But I respectfully implore those who reject my doctrine because they can make nothing of my stumbling language, to tell us in their own name — *und zwar* very concretely and articulately! — just how the real, genuine and absolutely 'objective' truth which they believe in so profoundly, *is* constituted and established. They must n't point to the 'reality' itself, for truth is only our subjective relation to realities. What is the nominal essence of this relation, its logical definition, whether or not it be 'objectively' attainable by mortals?

Whatever they may say it is, I have the firmest faith that my account will prove to

have allowed for it and included it by anticipation, as one possible case in the total mixture
of cases. There is, in short, no *room* for any
grade or sort of truth outside of the frame-
work of the pragmatic system, outside of that
jungle of empirical workings and leadings,
and their nearer or ulterior terminations, of
which I seem to have written so unskilfully.

VII

PROFESSOR PRATT ON TRUTH

I [1]

PROFESSOR J. B. PRATT'S paper in the *Journal of Philosophy* for June 6, 1907, is so brilliantly written that its misconception of the pragmatist position seems doubly to call for a reply.

He asserts that, for a pragmatist, truth cannot be a relation between an idea and a reality outside and transcendent of the idea, but must lie 'altogether within experience,' where it will need 'no reference to anything else to justify it' — no reference to the object, apparently. The pragmatist must 'reduce everything to psychology,' aye, and to the psychology of the immediate moment. He is consequently debarred from saying that an idea that eventually gets psychologically verified *was* already true before the process of verifying was com-

---

[1] Reprinted from the *Journal of Philosophy, etc.*, August 15, 1907 (vol. iv, p. 464).

plete; and he is equally debarred from treating an idea as true provisionally so long as he only believes that he *can* verify it whenever he will.

Whether such a pragmatist as this exists, I know not, never having myself met with the beast. We can define terms as we like; and if that be my friend Pratt's definition of a pragmatist, I can only concur with his anti-pragmatism. But, in setting up the weird type, he quotes words from me; so, in order to escape being classed by some reader along with so asinine a being, I will reassert my own view of truth once more.

Truth is essentially a relation between two things, an idea, on the one hand, and a reality outside of the idea, on the other. This relation, like all relations, has its *fundamentum*, namely, the matrix of experiential circumstance, psychological as well as physical, in which the correlated terms are found embedded. In the case of the relation between 'heir' and 'legacy' the *fundamentum* is a world in which there was a testator, and in which there is now a will and an executor; in the case of that between idea and object, it is a world with circumstances of a sort to make a satisfactory verification process, lying around and between the two terms. But just as a man may be called an heir and treated as one before the executor has divided the estate, so an idea may practically be credited with truth before the verification process has been exhaustively carried out — the existence of the mass of verifying circumstance is enough. Where potentiality counts for actuality in so many other cases, one does not see why it may not so count here. We call a man benevolent not only for his kind acts paid in, but for his readiness to perform others; we treat an idea as 'luminous' not only for the light it has shed, but for that we expect it will shed on dark problems. Why should we not equally trust the truth of our ideas? We live on credits everywhere; and we use our ideas far oftener for calling up things connected with their immediate objects, than for calling up those objects themselves. Ninety-nine times out of a hundred the only use we should make of the object itself, if we were led up to it by our idea, would be to pass on to those connected things by its means. So we continually curtail verification-processes, letting our belief that they are possible suffice.

What *constitutes the relation* known as truth, I now say, is just the *existence in the empirical world of this fundamentum of circumstance surrounding object and idea* and ready to be either short-circuited or traversed at full length. So long as it exists, and a satisfactory passage through it between the object and the idea is possible, that idea will both *be* true, and will *have been* true of that object, whether fully developed verification has taken place or not. The nature and place and affinities of the object of course play as vital a part in making the particular passage possible as do the nature and associative tendencies of the idea; so that the notion that truth could fall altogether inside of the thinker's private experience and be something purely psychological, is absurd. It is *between* the idea and the object that the truth-relation is to be sought and it involves both terms.

But the 'intellectualistic' position, if I understand Mr. Pratt rightly, is that, altho we can use this *fundamentum*, this mass of go-between experience, for *testing* truth, yet the truth-relation in itself remains as something apart. It means, in Mr. Pratt's words, merely *'this simple thing that the object of which one is thinking is as one thinks it.'*

It seems to me that the word 'as,' which qualifies the relation here, and bears the whole 'epistemological' burden, is anything but simple. What it most immediately suggests is that the idea should be *like* the object; but most of our ideas, being abstract concepts, bear almost no resemblance to their objects. The 'as' must therefore, I should say, be usually interpreted functionally, as meaning that the idea shall lead us into the same quarters of experience *as* the object would. Experience leads ever on and on, and objects and our ideas of objects may both lead to the same goals. The ideas being in that case shorter cuts, we *substitute* them more and more for their objects; and we habitually waive direct verification of each one of them, as their train passes through our mind, because if an idea leads *as* the object would lead, we can say, in Mr. Pratt's words, that in so far forth the object is *as* we think it, and that the idea, verified thus in so far forth, is true enough.

Mr. Pratt will undoubtedly accept most of these facts, but he will deny that they spell pragmatism. Of course, definitions are free to every one; but I have myself never meant by the pragmatic view of truth anything different from what I now describe; and inasmuch as my use of the term came earlier than my friend's, I think it ought to have the right of way. But I suspect that Professor Pratt's contention is not solely as to what one must think in order to be called a pragmatist. I am sure that he believes that the truth-relation has something *more* in it than the *fundamentum* which I assign can account for. Useful to test truth by, the matrix of circumstance, he thinks, cannot found the truth-relation *in se*, for that is trans-empirical and 'saltatory.'

Well, take an object and an idea, and assume that the latter is true of the former — as eternally and absolutely true as you like. Let the object be as much 'as' the idea thinks it, as it is possible for one thing to be 'as' another. I now formally ask of Professor Pratt to tell what this 'as'-ness in itself *consists* in — for it seems to me that it ought to consist in something assignable and describable, and not remain a pure mystery, and I promise that if he can assign any determination of it whatever which I cannot successfully refer to some specification of what in this article I have called the empirical *fundamentum*, I will confess my stupidity cheerfully, and will agree never to publish a line upon this subject of truth again.

II

Professor Pratt has returned to the charge in a whole book,[1] which for its clearness and good temper deserves to supersede all the rest

[1] J. B. Pratt: *What is Pragmatism*. New York, The Macmillan Company, 1909. — The comments I have printed were written in March, 1909, after some of the articles printed later in the present volume.

of the anti-pragmatistic literature. I wish it might do so; for its author admits all *my* essential contentions, simply distinguishing my account of truth as 'modified' pragmatism from Schiller's and Dewey's, which he calls pragmatism of the 'radical' sort. As I myself understand Dewey and Schiller, our views absolutely agree, in spite of our different modes of statement; but I have enough trouble of my own in life without having to defend my friends, so I abandon them provisionally to the tender mercy of Professor Pratt's interpretations, utterly erroneous tho I deem these to be. My reply as regards myself can be very short, for I prefer to consider only essentials, and Dr. Pratt's whole book hardly takes the matter farther than the article to which I retort in Part I of the present paper.

He repeats the 'as'-formula, as if it were something that I, along with other pragmatists, had denied,[1] whereas I have only asked those who insist so on its importance to do something more than merely utter it — to ex-

[1] *Op. cit.*, pp. 77–80.

plicate it, for example, and tell us what its so great importance consists in. I myself agree most cordially that for an idea to be true the object must be 'as' the idea declares it, but I explicate the 'as'-ness as meaning the idea's verifiability.

Now since Dr. Pratt denies none of these verifying 'workings' for which I have pleaded, but only insists on their inability to serve as the *fundamentum* of the truth-relation, it seems that there is really nothing in the line of *fact* about which we differ, and that the issue between us is solely as to how far the notion of workableness or verifiability is an essential part of the notion of 'trueness' — 'trueness' being Dr. Pratt's present name for the character of as-ness in the true idea. I maintain that there is no meaning left in this notion of as-ness or trueness if no reference to the possibility of concrete working on the part of the idea is made.

Take an example where there can be no possible working. Suppose I have an idea to which I give utterance by the vocable 'skrkl,' claiming at the same time that it is true. Who now can say that it is *false*, for why may there not be somewhere in the unplumbed depths of the cosmos some object with which 'skrkl' can agree and have trueness in Dr. Pratt's sense? On the other hand who can say that it is *true*, for who can lay his hand on that object and show that it and nothing else is what I *mean* by my word? But yet again, who can gainsay any one who shall call my word utterly *irrelative* to other reality, and treat it as a bare fact in my mind, devoid of any cognitive function whatever. One of these three alternatives must surely be predicated of it. For it not to be irrelevant (or not-cognitive in nature), an object of some kind must be provided which it may refer to. Supposing that object provided, whether 'skrkl' is true or false of it, depends, according to Professor Pratt, on no intermediating condition whatever. The trueness or the falsity is even now immediately, absolutely, and positively there.

I, on the other hand, demand a cosmic environment of some kind to establish which of

them is there rather than utter irrelevancy.[1]
I then say, first, that unless some sort of a natural path exists between the 'skrkl' and *that*
object, distinguishable among the innumerable pathways that run among all the realities
of the universe, linking them promiscuously
with one another, there is nothing there to constitute even the *possibility of its referring* to
that object rather than to any other.

I say furthermore that unless it have some
tendency to follow up that path, there is nothing to constitute its *intention* to refer to the
object in question.

[1] Dr. Pratt, singularly enough, disposes of this primal
postulate of all pragmatic epistemology, by saying that the
pragmatist 'unconsciously surrenders his whole case by smuggling in the idea of a conditioning environment which determines whether or not the experience can work, and which
cannot itself be identified with the experience or any part of
it' (pp. 167–168). The 'experience' means here of course the
idea, or belief; and the expression 'smuggling in' is to the last
degree diverting. If any epistemologist could dispense with
a conditioning environment, it would seem to be the anti-
pragmatist, with his immediate saltatory trueness, independent
of work done. The mediating pathway which the environment supplies is the very essence of the pragmatist's explanation.

Finally, I say that unless the path be strown with possibilities of frustration or encouragement, and offer some sort of terminal satisfaction or contradiction, there is nothing to constitute its *agreement* or *disagreement* with that object, or to constitute the as-ness (or 'not-asness') in which the trueness (or falseness) is said to consist.

I think that Dr. Pratt ought to do something more than repeat the name 'trueness,' in answer to my pathetic question whether that there be not some *constitution* to a relation as important as this. The pathway, the tendency, the corroborating or contradicting progress, need not in every case be experienced in full, but I don't see, if the universe does n't contain them among its possibilities of furniture, what *logical material for defining* the trueness of my idea is left. But if it do contain them, they and they only are the logical material required.

I am perplexed by the superior importance which Dr. Pratt attributes to abstract trueness over concrete verifiability in an idea, and I wish that he might be moved to explain. It is prior to verification, to be sure, but so is the verifiability for which I contend prior, just as a man's 'mortality' (which is nothing but the possibility of his death) is prior to his death, but it can hardly be that this abstract priority of all possibility to its correlative fact is what so obstinate a quarrel is about. I think it probable that Dr. Pratt is vaguely thinking of something concreter than this. The trueness of an idea must mean *something definite in it that determines its tendency to work*, and indeed towards this object rather than towards that. Undoubtedly there is something of this sort in the idea, just as there is something in man that accounts for his tendency towards death, and in bread that accounts for its tendency to nourish. What that something is in the case of truth psychology tells us: the idea has associates peculiar to itself, motor as well as ideational; it tends by its place and nature to call these into being, one after another; and the appearance of them in succession is what we mean by the 'workings' of the idea. According to what they are, does the trueness or falseness which the idea harbored come to light. These tendencies have still earlier conditions which, in a general way, biology, psychology and biography can trace. This whole chain of natural causal conditions produces a resultant state of things in which new relations, not simply causal, can now be found, or into which they can now be introduced, — the relations namely which we epistemologists study, relations of adaptation, of substitutability, of instrumentality, of reference and of truth.

The prior causal conditions, altho there could be no knowing of any kind, true or false, without them, are but preliminary to the question of what makes the ideas true or false when once their tendencies have been obeyed. The tendencies must exist in some shape anyhow, but their fruits are truth, falsity, or irrelevancy, according to what they concretely turn out to be. They are not 'saltatory' at any rate, for they evoke their consequences contiguously, from next to next only; and not until the final result of the whole associative sequence, actual or potential, is in our mental sight, can we feel sure what its epistemological significance, if it have any, may be. True knowing is, in fine, not substantially, in itself, or 'as such,' inside of the idea from the first, any more than mortality *as such* is inside of the man, or nourishment *as such* inside of the bread. Something else is there first, that practically *makes for* knowing, dying or nourishing, as the case may be. That something is the 'nature' namely of the first term, be it idea, man, or bread, that operates to start the causal chain of processes which, when completed, is the complex fact to which we give whatever functional name best fits the case, Another nature, another chain of cognitive workings; and then either another object known or the same object known differently, will ensue.

Dr. Pratt perplexes me again by seeming to charge Dewey and Schiller [1] (I am not sure that he charges me) with an account of truth which would allow the object believed in not to exist, even if the belief in it were true. 'Since

---

[1] Page 200.

the truth of an idea,' he writes, 'means merely
the fact that the idea works, that fact is all
that you mean when you say the idea is true'
(p. 206). '*When you say the idea is true*' —
does that mean true for *you*, the critic, or true
for the believer whom you are describing?
The critic's trouble over this seems to come
from his taking the word 'true' irrelatively,
whereas the pragmatist always means 'true
for him who experiences the workings.' 'But
is the object *really* true or not?' — the critic
then seems to ask, — as if the pragmatist were
bound to throw in a whole ontology on top of
his epistemology and tell us what realities in-
dubitably exist. 'One world at a time,' would
seem to be the right reply here.

One other trouble of Dr. Pratt's must be noticed. It concerns the 'transcendence' of the
object. When our ideas have worked so as to
bring us flat up against the object, *next* to it,
'is our relation to it then ambulatory or saltatory?' Dr. Pratt asks. If *your* headache be
my object, '*my* experiences break off where
yours begin,' Dr. Pratt writes, and 'this fact

is of great importance, for it bars out the sense
of transition and fulfilment which forms so
important an element in the pragmatist description of knowledge — the sense of fulfilment due to a continuous passage from the
original idea to the known object. If this comes
at all when I know your headache, it comes
not with the object, but quite on my side of the
"epistemological gulf." The gulf is still there
to be transcended " (p. 158).

Some day of course, or even now somewhere in the larger life of the universe, different men's headaches may become confluent
or be 'co-conscious.' Here and now, however,
headaches do transcend each other and, when
not felt, can be known only conceptually. My
idea is that you really have a headache; it
works well with what I see of your expression,
and with what I hear you say; but it does n't
put me in possession of the headache itself.
I am still at one remove, and the headache
'transcends' me, even tho it be in nowise
transcendent of human experience generally.
But the 'gulf' here is that which the pragma-

tist epistemology itself fixes in the very first words it uses, by saying there must be an object and an idea. The idea however does n't immediately leap the gulf, it only works from next to next so as to bridge it, fully or approximately. If it bridges it, in the pragmatist's vision of his hypothetical universe, it can be called a 'true' idea. If it only *might* bridge it, but does n't, or if it throws a bridge distinctly *at* it, it still has, in the onlooking pragmatist's eyes, what Professor Pratt calls 'trueness.' But to ask the pragmatist thereupon whether, when it thus fails to coalesce bodily with the object, it is *really* true or has *real* trueness, — in other words whether the headache he supposes, and supposes the thinker he supposes, to believe in, be a real headache or not, — is to step from his hypothetical universe of discourse into the altogether different world of natural fact.

VIII

THE PRAGMATIST ACCOUNT OF TRUTH AND ITS MISUNDER- STANDERS[1]

THE account of truth given in my volume entitled *Pragmatism*, continues to meet with such persistent misunderstanding that I am tempted to make a final brief reply. My ideas may well deserve refutation, but they can get none till they are conceived of in their proper shape. The fantastic character of the current misconceptions shows how unfamiliar is the concrete point of view which pragmatism assumes. Persons who are familiar with a conception move about so easily in it that they understand each other at a hint, and can converse without anxiously attending to their P's and Q's. I have to admit, in view of the results, that we have assumed too ready an intelligence, and consequently in many places

[1] Reprint from the *Philosophical Review*, January, 1908 (vol. xvii, p. 1).

used a language too slipshod. We should never have spoken elliptically. The critics have boggled at every word they could boggle at, and refused to take the spirit rather than the letter of our discourse. This seems to show a genuine unfamiliarity in the whole point of view. It also shows, I think, that the second stage of opposition, which has already begun to express itself in the stock phrase that 'what is new is not true, and what is true not new,' in pragmatism, is insincere. If we said nothing in any degree new, why was our meaning so desperately hard to catch? The blame cannot be laid wholly upon our obscurity of speech, for in other subjects we have attained to making ourselves understood. But recriminations are tasteless; and, as far as I personally am concerned, I am sure that some of the misconception I complain of is due to my doctrine of truth being surrounded in that volume of popular lectures by a lot of other opinions not necessarily implicated with it, so that a reader may very naturally have grown confused. For this I am to blame, — likewise for omitting certain explicit cautions, which the pages that follow will now in part supply.

First misunderstanding: Pragmatism is only a re-editing of positivism.

This seems the commonest mistake. Scepticism, positivism, and agnosticism agree with ordinary dogmatic rationalism in presupposing that everybody knows what the word 'truth' means, without further explanation. But the former doctrines then either suggest or declare that real truth, absolute truth, is inaccessible to us, and that we must fain put up with relative or phenomenal truth as its next best substitute. By scepticism this is treated as an unsatisfactory state of affairs, while positivism and agnosticism are cheerful about it, call real truth sour grapes, and consider phenomenal truth quite sufficient for all our 'practical' purposes.

In point of fact, nothing could be farther from all this than what pragmatism has to say of truth. Its thesis is an altogether previous one. It leaves off where these other theories begin, having contented itself with the word truth's *definition*. 'No matter whether any mind extant in the universe possess truth or not,' it asks, 'what does the notion of truth signify *ideally?*' 'What kind of things would true judgments be *in case* they existed?' The answer which pragmatism offers is intended to cover the most complete truth that can be conceived of, 'absolute' truth if you like, as well as truth of the most relative and imperfect description. This question of what truth would be like if it did exist, belongs obviously to a purely speculative field of inquiry. It is not a theory about any sort of reality, or about what kind of knowledge is actually possible; it abstracts from particular terms altogether, and defines the nature of a possible relation between two of them.

As Kant's question about synthetic judgments had escaped previous philosophers, so the pragmatist question is not only so subtile as to have escaped attention hitherto, but even so subtile, it would seem, that when openly broached now, dogmatists and sceptics alike fail to apprehend it, and deem the pragmatist to be treating of something wholly different. He insists, they say (I quote an actual critic), 'that the greater problems are insoluble by human intelligence, that our need of knowing truly is artificial and illusory, and that our reason, incapable of reaching the foundations of reality, must turn itself exclusively towards *action*.' There could not be a worse misapprehension.

Second misunderstanding: Pragmatism is primarily an appeal to action.

The name 'pragmatism,' with its suggestions of action, has been an unfortunate choice, I have to admit, and has played into the hands of this mistake. But no word could protect the doctrine from critics so blind to the nature of the inquiry that, when Dr. Schiller speaks of ideas 'working' well, the only thing they think of is their immediate workings in the physical environment, their enabling us to make money, or gain some similar 'practical' advantage. Ideas do work thus, of course, immediately or remotely; but they work indefinitely inside of the mental world also. Not crediting us with this rudimentary insight, our critics treat our view as offering itself exclusively to engineers, doctors, financiers, and men of action generally, who need some sort of a rough and ready *weltanschauung*, but have no time or wit to study genuine philosophy. It is usually described as a characteristically American movement, a sort of bobtailed scheme of thought, excellently fitted for the man on the street, who naturally hates theory and wants cash returns immediately.

It is quite true that, when the refined theoretic question that pragmatism begins with is once answered, secondary corollaries of a practical sort follow. Investigation shows that, in the function called truth, previous realities are not the only independent variables. To a certain extent our ideas, being realities, are also independent variables, and, just as they follow other reality and fit it, so, in a measure, does other reality follow and fit them. When they add themselves to being, they partly redetermine the existent, so that reality as a whole appears incompletely definable unless ideas also are kept account of. This pragmatist doctrine, exhibiting our ideas as complemental factors of reality, throws open (since our ideas are instigators of our action) a wide window upon human action, as well as a wide license to originality in thought. But few things could be sillier than to ignore the prior epistemological edifice in which the window is built, or to talk as if pragmatism began and ended at the window. This, nevertheless, is what our critics do almost without exception. They ignore our primary step and its motive, and make the relation to action, which is our secondary achievement, primary.

Third misunderstanding: Pragmatists cut themselves off from the right to believe in ejective realities.

They do so, according to the critics, by making the truth of our beliefs consist in their verifiability, and their verifiability in the way in which they do work for us. Professor Stout, in his otherwise admirable and hopeful review of Schiller in *Mind* for October, 1897, considers that this ought to lead Schiller (could he sincerely realize the effects of his own doctrine) to the absurd consequence of being unable to believe genuinely in another man's headache, even were the headache there. He can only 'postulate' it for the sake of the working value of the postulate to himself. The postulate guides certain of his acts and leads to advantageous consequences; but the moment he understands fully that the postulate is true *only* (!) in this sense, it ceases (or should cease) to be true for him that the other man really *has* a headache. All that makes the postulate most precious then evaporates: his interest in his fellow-man 'becomes a veiled form of self-interest, and his world grows cold, dull, and heartless.'

Such an objection makes a curious muddle of the pragmatist's universe of discourse. Within that universe the pragmatist finds some one with a headache or other feeling, and some one else who postulates that feeling. Asking on what condition the postulate is 'true,' the pragmatist replies that, for the postulator at any rate, it is true just in proportion as to believe in it works in him the fuller sum of satisfactions. What is it that is satisfactory here? Surely to *believe* in the postulated object, namely, in the really existing feeling of the other man. But how (especially if the postulator were himself a thoroughgoing pragmatist) could it ever be satisfactory to him *not* to believe in that feeling, so long as, in Professor Stout's words, disbelief 'made the world seem to him cold, dull, and heartless'? Disbelief would seem, on pragmatist principles, quite out of the question under such conditions, unless the heartlessness of the world were made probable already on other grounds. And since the belief in the headache, true for the subject assumed in the pragmatist's universe of discourse, is also true for the pragmatist who for his epitemologizing purposes has assumed that entire universe, why is it not true in that universe absolutely? The headache believed in is a reality there, and no extant mind disbelieves it, neither the critic's mind nor his subject's! Have our opponents any better brand of truth in this real universe of ours that they can show us?[1]

[1] I see here a chance to forestall a criticism which some one may make on Lecture III of my *Pragmatism*, where, on pp. 96-100, I said that 'God' and 'Matter' might be regarded as synonymous terms, so long as no differing future consequences were deducible from the two conceptions. The passage was transcribed from my address at the California Philosophical Union, reprinted in the *Journal of Philosophy*, vol. i, p. 673. I had no sooner given the address than I perceived a flaw in that part of it; but I have left the passage unaltered ever since, because the flaw did not spoil its illustrative value. The flaw was evident when, as a case analogous to that of a godless universe, I thought of what I called an 'automatic sweetheart,' meaning a soulless body which should be absolutely indistinguishable from a spiritually animated maiden, laughing, talking, blushing, nursing us, and performing all feminine offices as tactfully and sweetly as if a soul were in her. Would any one regard her as a full equivalent? Certainly not, and why? Because, framed as we are, our egoism craves above all things inward sympathy and recognition, love and admiration. The outward treatment is valued mainly as an expression, as a manifestation of the accompanying consciousness believed in. Pragmatically, then, belief in the automatic sweetheart would not *work*, and in point of fact no one treats it as a serious hypothesis. The godless universe would be exactly similar. Even if matter could do every outward thing that God does, the idea of it would not work as satisfactorily, because the chief call for a God on modern men's part is for a being who will

So much for the third misunderstanding, which is but one specification of the following still wider one.

Fourth misunderstanding: No pragmatist can be a realist in his epistemology.

This is supposed to follow from his statement that the truth of our beliefs consists in general in their giving satisfaction. Of course satisfaction *per se* is a subjective condition; so the conclusion is drawn that truth falls wholly inside of the subject, who then may manufacture it at his pleasure. True beliefs become thus wayward affections, severed from all responsibility to other parts of experience.

It is difficult to excuse such a parody of the pragmatist's opinion, ignoring as it does every element but one of his universe of discourse. The terms of which that universe consists positively forbid any non-realistic interpretation of the function of knowledge defined there.

inwardly recognize them and judge them sympathetically. Matter disappoints this craving of our ego, so God remains for most men the truer hypothesis, and indeed remains so for definite pragmatic reasons.

The pragmatizing epistemologist posits there a reality and a mind with ideas. What, now, he asks, can make those ideas true of that reality? Ordinary epistemology contents itself with the vague statement that the ideas must 'correspond' or 'agree'; the pragmatist insists on being more concrete, and asks what such 'agreement' may mean in detail. He finds first that the ideas must point to or lead towards *that* reality and no other, and then that the pointings and leadings must yield satisfaction as their result. So far the pragmatist is hardly less abstract than the ordinary slouchy epistemologist; but as he defines himself farther, he grows more concrete. The entire quarrel of the intellectualist with him is over his concreteness, intellectualism contending that the vaguer and more abstract account is here the more profound. The concrete pointing and leading are conceived by the pragmatist to be the work of other portions of the same universe to which the reality and the mind belong, intermediary verifying bits of experience with which the mind at one end, and the reality at the other, are joined. The 'satisfaction,' in turn, is no abstract satisfaction *überhaupt*, felt by an unspecified being, but is assumed to consist of such satisfactions (in the plural) as concretely existing men actually do find in their beliefs. As we humans are constituted in point of fact, we find that to believe in other men's minds, in independent physical realities, in past events, in eternal logical relations, is satisfactory. We find hope satisfactory. We often find it satisfactory to cease to doubt. Above all we find *consistency* satisfactory, consistency between the present idea and the entire rest of our mental equipment, including the whole order of our sensations, and that of our intuitions of likeness and difference, and our whole stock of previously acquired truths.

The pragmatist, being himself a man, and imagining in general no contrary lines of truer belief than ours about the 'reality' which he has laid at the base of his epistemological discussion, is willing to treat our satisfactions as possibly really true guides to it, not as guides true solely for *us*. It would seem here to be the duty of his critics to show with some explicitness why, being our subjective feelings, these satisfactions can *not* yield 'objective' truth. The beliefs which they accompany 'posit' the assumed reality, 'correspond' and 'agree' with it, and 'fit' it in perfectly definite and assignable ways, through the sequent trains of thought and action which form their verification, so merely to insist on using these words abstractly instead of concretely is no way of driving the pragmatist from the field, — his more concrete account virtually includes his critic's. If our critics have any definite idea of a truth more objectively grounded than the kind we propose, why do they not show it more articulately? As they stand, they remind one of Hegel's man who wanted 'fruit,' but rejected cherries, pears, and grapes, because they were not fruit in the abstract. We offer them the full quart-pot, and they cry for the empty quart-capacity.

But here I think I hear some critic retort as follows: 'If satisfactions are all that is needed to make truth, how about the notorious fact that errors are so often satisfactory? And how about the equally notorious fact that certain true beliefs may cause the bitterest dissatisfaction? Is n't it clear that not the satisfaction which it gives, but the relation of the belief *to the reality* is all that makes it true? Suppose there were no such reality, and that the satisfactions yet remained: would they not then effectively work falsehood? Can they consequently be treated distinctively as the truth-builders? It is the *inherent relation to reality* of a belief that gives us that specific *truth*-satisfaction, compared with which all other satisfactions are the hollowest humbug. The satisfaction of *knowing truly* is thus the only one which the pragmatist ought to have considered. As a *psychological sentiment*, the anti-pragmatist gladly concedes it to him, but then only as a concomitant of truth, not as a constituent. What *constitutes* truth is not the sentiment, but the purely logical or objective function of rightly cognizing the reality, and the pragmatist's failure to reduce this function to lower values is patent.'

Such anti-pragmatism as this seems to me a tissue of confusion. To begin with, when the pragmatist says 'indispensable,' it confounds this with 'sufficient.' The pragmatist calls satisfactions indispensable for truth-building, but I have everywhere called them insufficient unless reality be also incidentally led to. If the reality assumed were cancelled from the pragmatist's universe of discourse, he would straightway give the name of falsehoods to the beliefs remaining, in spite of all their satisfactoriness. For him, as for his critic, there can be no truth if there is nothing to be true about. Ideas are so much flat psychological surface unless some mirrored matter gives them cognitive lustre. This is why as a pragmatist I have so carefully posited 'reality' *ab initio*, and why, throughout my whole discussion, I remain an epistemological realist.[1]

The anti-pragmatist is guilty of the further

---

[1] I need hardly remind the reader that both sense-percepts and percepts of ideal relation (comparisons, etc.) should be classed among the realities. The bulk of our mental 'stock' consists of truths concerning these terms.

confusion of imagining that, in undertaking to give him an account of what truth formally means, we are assuming at the same time to provide a warrant for it, trying to define the occasions when he can be sure of materially possessing it. Our making it hinge on a reality so 'independent' that when it comes, truth comes, and when it goes, truth goes with it, disappoints this *naïve* expectation, so he deems our description unsatisfactory. I suspect that under this confusion lies the still deeper one of not discriminating sufficiently between the two notions, truth and reality. Realities are not *true*, they *are;* and beliefs are true *of* them. But I suspect that in the anti-pragmatist mind the two notions sometimes swap their attributes. The reality itself, I fear, is treated as if 'true,' and conversely. Whoso tells us of the one, it is then supposed, must also be telling us of the other; and a true idea must in a manner *be*, or at least *yield* without extraneous aid, the reality it cognitively is possessed of.

To this absolute-idealistic demand pragmatism simply opposes its *non possumus.* If there is to be truth, it says, both realities and beliefs about them must conspire to make it; but whether there ever is such a thing, or how anyone can be sure that his own beliefs possess it, it never pretends to determine. That truth-satisfaction *par excellence* which may tinge a belief unsatisfactory in other ways, it easily explains as the feeling of consistency with the stock of previous truths, or supposed truths, of which one's whole past experience may have left one in possession.

But are not all pragmatists sure that their own belief is right? their enemies will ask at this point; and this leads me to the

Fifth misunderstanding: What pragmatists say is inconsistent with their saying so.

A correspondent puts this objection as follows: 'When you say to your audience, "pragmatism is the truth concerning truth," the first truth is different from the second. About the first you and they are not to be at odds; you are not giving them liberty to take or leave it according as it works satisfactorily or not for their private uses. Yet the second truth, which ought to describe and include the first, affirms this liberty. Thus the *intent* of your utterance seems to contradict the *content* of it.'

General scepticism has always received this same classic refutation. 'You have to dogmatize,' the rationalists say to the sceptics, 'whenever you express the sceptical position; so your lives keep contradicting your thesis.' One would suppose that the impotence of so hoary an argument to abate in the slightest degree the amount of general scepticism in the world might have led some rationalists themselves to doubt whether these instantaneous logical refutations are such fatal ways, after all, of killing off live mental attitudes. General scepticism is the live mental attitude of refusing to conclude. It is a permanent torpor of the will, renewing itself in detail towards each successive thesis that offers, and you can no more kill it off by logic than you can kill off obstinacy or practical joking. This is why it is so irritating. Your consistent sceptic never puts his scepticism into a formal proposition, — he simply chooses it as a habit. He provokingly hangs back when he might so easily join us in saying yes, but he is not illogical or stupid, — on the contrary, he often impresses us by his intellectual superiority. This is the *real* scepticism that rationalists have to meet, and their logic does not even touch it.

No more can logic kill the pragmatist's behavior: his act of utterance, so far from contradicting, accurately exemplifies the matter which he utters. What is the matter which he utters? In part, it is this, that truth, concretely considered, is an attribute of our beliefs, and that these are attitudes that follow satisfactions. The ideas around which the satisfactions cluster are primarily only hypotheses that challenge or summon a belief to come and take its stand upon them. The pragmatist's idea of truth is just such a challenge. He finds it ultra-satisfactory to accept it, and takes his own stand accordingly. But, being gregarious as they are, men seek to spread their beliefs, to awaken imitation, to infect others. Why should not *you* also find the same belief satisfactory? thinks the pragmatist, and forthwith endeavors to convert you. You and he will then believe similarly; you will hold up your subject-end of a truth, which will be a truth objective and irreversible if the reality holds up the object-end by being itself present simultaneously. What there is of self-contradiction in all this I confess I cannot discover. The pragmatist's conduct in his own case seems to me on the contrary admirably to illustrate his universal formula; and of all epistemologists, he is perhaps the only one who is irreproachably self-consistent.

Sixth misunderstanding: Pragmatism explains not what truth is, but only how it is arrived at.

In point of fact it tells us both, tells us what it is incidentally to telling us how it is arrived at, — for what *is* arrived at except just what the truth is? If I tell you how to get to the railroad station, don't I implicitly introduce you to the *what*, to the being and nature of that edifice? It is quite true that the abstract *word* 'how' has n't the same meaning as the abstract *word* 'what,' but in this universe of concrete facts you cannot keep hows and whats asunder. The reasons why I find it satisfactory to believe that any idea is true, the *how* of my arriving at that belief, may be among the very reasons why the idea *is* true in reality. If not, I summon the anti-pragmatist to explain the impossibility articulately.

His trouble seems to me mainly to arise from his fixed inability to understand how a concrete statement can possibly mean as much, or be as valuable, as an abstract one. I said above that the main quarrel between us and our critics was that of concreteness *versus* abstractness. This is the place to develop that point farther.

In the present question, the links of experience sequent upon an idea, which mediate between it and a reality, form and for the pragmatist indeed *are,* the *concrete* relation of truth that may obtain between the idea and that reality. They, he says, are all that we mean when we speak of the idea 'pointing' to the reality, 'fitting' it, 'corresponding' with it, or 'agreeing' with it, — they or other similar mediating trains of verification. Such mediating events *make* the idea 'true.' The idea itself, if it exists at all, is also a concrete event: so pragmatism insists that truth in the singular is only a collective name for truths in the plural, these consisting always of series of definite events; and that what intellectualism calls *the* truth, the *inherent* truth, of any one such series is only the abstract name for its truthfulness in act, for the fact that the ideas there do lead to the supposed reality in a way that we consider satisfactory.

The pragmatist himself has no objection to abstractions. Elliptically, and 'for short,' he relies on them as much as any one, finding upon innumerable occasions that their comparative emptiness makes of them useful substitutes for the overfulness of the facts he meets with. But he never ascribes to them a higher grade of reality. The full reality of a truth for him is always some process of verification, in which the abstract property of connecting ideas with objects truly is workingly embodied. Meanwhile it is endlessly serviceable to be able to talk of properties abstractly and apart from their working, to find them the same in innumerable cases, to take them 'out of time,' and to treat of their relations to other similar abstractions. We thus form whole universes of platonic ideas *ante rem*, universes *in posse*, tho none of them exists effectively except *in rebus*. Countless relations obtain there which nobody experiences as obtaining, — as, in the eternal universe of musical relations, for example, the notes of Aennchen von Tharau were a lovely melody long ere mortal ears ever heard them. Even so the music of the future sleeps now, to be awakened hereafter. Or, if we take the world of geometrical relations, the thousandth decimal of π sleeps there, tho no one may ever try to compute it. Or, if we take the universe of 'fitting,' countless coats 'fit' backs, and countless boots 'fit' feet, on which they are not practically *fitted;* countless stones 'fit' gaps in walls into which no one seeks to fit them actually. In the same way countless opinions 'fit' realities, and countless truths are valid, tho no thinker ever thinks them.

For the anti-pragmatist these prior timeless relations are the presupposition of the concrete ones, and possess the profounder dignity and value. The actual workings of our ideas in verification-processes are as naught in comparison with the 'obtainings' of this discarnate truth within them.

For the pragmatist, on the contrary, all discarnate truth is static, impotent, and relatively spectral, full truth being the truth that energizes and does battle. Can any one suppose that the sleeping quality of truth would ever have been abstracted or have received a name, if truths had remained forever in that storage-vault of essential timeless 'agreements' and had never been embodied in any panting struggle of men's live ideas for verification? Surely no more than the abstract property of 'fitting' would have received a name, if in our world there had been no backs or feet or gaps in walls to be actually fitted. *Existential* truth is incidental to the actual competition of opinions. *Essential* truth, the truth of the intellectualists, the truth with no one thinking it, is like the coat that fits tho no one has ever tried it on, like the music that no ear has listened to. It is less real, not more real, than the verified article; and to attribute a superior degree of glory to it seems little more than a piece of perverse abstraction-worship. As well might a pencil insist that the outline is the essential thing in all pictorial representation, and chide the paint-brush and the camera for omitting it, forgetting that *their* pictures not only contain the whole outline, but a hundred other things in addition. Pragmatist truth contains the whole of intellectualist truth and a hundred other things in addition. Intellectualist truth is then only pragmatist truth *in posse*. That on innumerable occasions men do substitute truth *in posse* or verifiability, for verification or truth in act, is a fact to which no one attributes more importance than the pragmatist: he emphasizes the practical utility of such a habit. But he does not on that account consider truth *in posse*, — truth not alive enough ever to have been asserted or questioned or contradicted, — to be the metaphysically prior thing, to which truths in act are tributary and subsidiary. When intellectualists do this, pragmatism charges them with inverting the real relation. Truth in posse *means* only truths in act; and he insists that these latter take precedence in the order of logic as well as in that of being.

Seventh misunderstanding: Pragmatism ignores the theoretic interest.

This would seem to be an absolutely wanton slander, were not a certain excuse to be found in the linguistic affinities of the word 'pragmatism,' and in certain offhand habits of speech of ours which assumed too great a generosity on our reader's part. When we spoke of the meaning of ideas consisting in their 'practical' consequences, or of the 'practical' differences which our beliefs make to us; when we said that the truth of a belief consists in its 'working' value, etc.; our language evidently was too careless, for by 'practical' we were almost unanimously held to mean *opposed* to theoretical or genuinely cognitive, and the consequence was punctually drawn that a truth in our eyes could have no relation to any independent reality, or to any other truth, or to anything whatever but the acts which we might ground on it or the satisfactions they might bring. The mere existence of the idea, all by itself, if only its results were satisfactory, would give full truth to it, it was charged, in our absurd pragmatist epistemology. The solemn attribution of this rubbish to us was also encouraged by two other circumstances. First, ideas *are* practically useful in the narrow sense, false ideas sometimes, but most often ideas which we can verify by the sum total of all their leadings, and the reality of whose objects may thus be considered established beyond doubt. That these ideas should be true in advance of and apart from their utility, that, in other words, their objects should be really there, is the very condition of their having that

kind of utility, — the objects they connect us
with are so important that the ideas which serve
as the objects' substitutes grow important also.
This manner of their practical working was the
first thing that made truths good in the eyes of
primitive men; and buried among all the other
good workings by which true beliefs are char-
acterized, this kind of subsequential utility
remains.

The second misleading circumstance was
the emphasis laid by Schiller and Dewey on
the fact that, unless a truth be relevant to the
mind's momentary predicament, unless it be
germane to the 'practical' situation, — meaning by this the quite particular perplexity, —
it is no good to urge it. It does n't meet our
interests any better than a falsehood would
under the same circumstances. But why our
predicaments and perplexities might not be
theoretical here as well as narrowly practical,
I wish that our critics would explain. They
simply assume that no pragmatist *can* admit
a genuinely theoretic interest. Having used
the phrase 'cash-value' of an idea, I am im-

plored by one correspondent to alter it, 'for every one thinks you mean only pecuniary profit and loss.' Having said that the true is 'the expedient in our thinking,' I am rebuked in this wise by another learned correspondent: 'The word expedient has no other meaning than that of self-interest. The pursuit of this has ended by landing a number of officers of national banks in penitentiaries. A philosophy that leads to such results must be unsound.'

But the word 'practical' is so habitually loosely used that more indulgence might have been expected. When one says that a sick man has now practically recovered, or that an enterprise has practically failed, one usually means just the opposite of practically in the literal sense. One means that, altho untrue in strict practice, what one says is true in theory, true virtually, *certain to be* true. Again, by the practical one often means the distinctively concrete, the individual, particular, and effective, as opposed to the abstract, general, and inert. To speak for myself, whenever I have emphasized the practical nature of truth, this is mainly what has been in my mind. 'Pragmata' are things in their plurality; and in that early California address, when I described pragmatism as holding that 'the meaning of any proposi-- tion can always be brought down to some particular consequence in our future practical experience, whether passive or active,' I expressly added these qualifying words: 'the point lying rather in the fact that the experience must be particular than in the fact that it must be active,' — by 'active' meaning here 'practical' in the narrow literal sense.[1] But particular consequences can perfectly well be of a theo-

---

[1] The ambiguity of the word 'practical' comes out well in these words of a recent would-be reporter of our views: 'Pragmatism is an Anglo-Saxon reaction against the intellectualism and rationalism of the Latin mind. . . . Man, each individual man is the measure of things. He is able to conceive none but relative truths, that is to say, illusions. What these illusions are worth is revealed to him, not by general theory, but by individual practice. Pragmatism, which consists in experiencing these illusions of the mind and obeying them by acting them out, is a *philosophy without words*, a philosophy of *gestures and of acts*, which abandons what is general and holds only to what is *particular*.' (Bourdeau, in *Journal des Débats*, October 29, 1907.)

retic nature. Every remote fact which we infer from an idea is a particular theoretic consequence which our mind practically works towards. The loss of every old opinion of ours which we see that we shall have to give up if a new opinion be true, is a particular theoretic as well as a particular practical consequence. After man's interest in breathing freely, the greatest of all his interests (because it never fluctuates or remits, as most of his physical interests do), is his interest in *consistency*, in feeling that what he now thinks goes with what he thinks on other occasions. We tirelessly compare truth with truth for this sole purpose. Is the present candidate for belief perhaps contradicted by principle number one? Is it compatible with fact number two? and so forth. The particular operations here are the purely logical ones of analysis, deduction, comparison, etc.; and altho general terms may be used *ad libitum*, the satisfactory *practical working* of the candidate-idea consists in the consciousness yielded by each successive theoretic consequence in particular. It is therefore simply idiotic to repeat that pragmatism takes no account of purely theoretic interests. All it insists on is that verity in act means *verifications*, and that these are always particulars. Even in exclusively theoretic matters, it insists that vagueness and generality serve to verify nothing.

Eighth misunderstanding: Pragmatism is shut up to solipsism.

I have already said something about this misconception under the third and fourth heads, above, but a little more may be helpful. The objection is apt to clothe itself in words like these: 'You make truth to consist in every value except the cognitive value proper; you always leave your knower at many removes (or, at the uttermost, at one remove) from his real object; the best you do is to let his ideas carry him towards it; it remains forever outside of him,' etc.

I think that the leaven working here is the rooted intellectualist persuasion that, to know a reality, an idea must in some inscrutable fashion possess or be it.[1] For pragmatism this kind of coalescence is inessential. As a rule our cognitions are only processes of mind off their balance and in motion towards real termini; and the reality of the termini, believed in by the states of mind in question, can be *guaranteed* only by some wider knower.[2] But

---

[1] Sensations may, indeed, possess their objects or coalesce with them, as common sense supposes that they do; and intuited differences between concepts may coalesce with the 'eternal' objective differences; but to simplify our discussion here we can afford to abstract from these very special cases of knowing.

[2] The transcendental idealist thinks that, in some inexplicable way, the finite states of mind are identical with the transfinite all-knower which he finds himself obliged to postulate in order to supply a *fundamentum* for the relation of knowing, as he apprehends it. Pragmatists can leave the question of identity open; but they cannot do without the wider knower any more than they can do without the reality, if they want to *prove* a case of knowing. They themselves play the part of the absolute knower for the universe of discourse which serves them as material for epistemologizing. They warrant the reality there, and the subject's true knowledge, there, of it. But whether what they themselves say about that whole universe is objectively true, *i. e.*, whether the pragmatic theory of truth is true *really*, they cannot warrant, — they can only believe it. To their hearers they can only *propose* it, as I propose it to my readers, as something to be verified *ambulando*, or by the way in which its consequences may confirm it.

if there is no reason extant in the universe why they should be doubted, the beliefs are true in the only sense in which anything can be true anyhow: they are practically and concretely true, namely. True in the mystical mongrel sense of an *Identitätsphilosophie* they need not be; nor is there any intelligible reason why they ever need be true otherwise than verifiably and practically. It is reality's part to possess its own existence; it is thought's part to get into 'touch' with it by innumerable paths of verification.

I fear that the 'humanistic' developments of pragmatism may cause a certain difficulty here. We get at one truth only through the rest of truth; and the reality, everlastingly postulated as that which all our truth must keep in touch with, may never be given to us save in the form of truth other than that which we are now testing. But since Dr. Schiller has shown that all our truths, even the most elemental, are affected by race-inheritance with a human co-efficient, reality *per se* thus may appear only as a sort of limit; it may be held to shrivel to the mere *place* for an object, and what is known may be held to be only matter of our psyche that we fill the place with.

It must be confessed that pragmatism, worked in this humanistic way, is *compatible* with solipsism. It joins friendly hands with the agnostic part of kantism, with contemporary agnosticism, and with idealism generally. But worked thus, it is a metaphysical theory about the matter of reality, and flies far beyond pragmatism's own modest analysis of the nature of the knowing function, which analysis may just as harmoniously be combined with less humanistic accounts of reality. One of pragmatism's merits is that it is so purely epistemological. It must assume realities; but it prejudges nothing as to their constitution, and the most diverse metaphysics can use it as their foundation. It certainly has no special affinity with solipsism.

As I look back over what I have written, much of it gives me a queer impression, as if the obvious were set forth so condescendingly that readers might well laugh at my pomposity. It may be, however, that concreteness as radical as ours is not so obvious. The whole originality of pragmatism, the whole point in it, is its use of the concrete way of seeing. It begins with concreteness, and returns and ends with it. Dr. Schiller, with his two 'practical' aspects of truth, (1) relevancy to situation, and (2) subsequential utility, is only filling the cup of concreteness to the brim for us. Once seize that cup, and you cannot misunderstand pragmatism. It seems as if the power of imagining the world concretely *might* have been common enough to let our readers apprehend us better, as if they might have read between our lines, and, in spite of all our infelicities of expression, guessed a little more correctly what our thought was. But alas! this was not on fate's programme, so we can only think, with the German ditty : —

> "Es wär' zu schön gewesen,
> Es hat nicht sollen sein."

IX

THE MEANING OF THE WORD TRUTH[1]

My account of truth is realistic, and follows the epistemological dualism of common sense. Suppose I say to you 'The thing exists' — is that true or not? How can you tell? Not till my statement has developed its meaning farther is it determined as being true, false, or irrelevant to reality altogether. But if now you ask 'what thing?' and I reply 'a desk'; if you ask 'where?' and I point to a place; if you ask 'does it exist materially, or only in imagination?' and I say 'materially'; if moreover I say 'I mean that desk,' and then grasp and shake a desk which you see just as I have described it, you are willing to call my statement true. But you and I are commutable here; we can exchange places; and, as you go bail for my desk, so I can go bail for yours.

This notion of a reality independent of

[1] Remarks at the meeting of the American Philosophical Association, Cornell University, December, 1907.

either of us, taken from ordinary social experience, lies at the base of the pragmatist definition of truth. With some such reality any statement, in order to be counted true, must agree. Pragmatism defines 'agreeing' to mean certain ways of 'working,' be they actual or potential. Thus, for my statement 'the desk exists' to be true of a desk recognized as real by you, it must be able to lead me to shake your desk, to explain myself by words that suggest that desk to your mind, to make a drawing that is like the desk you see, etc. Only in such ways as this is there sense in saying it agrees with *that* reality, only thus does it gain for me the satisfaction of hearing you corroborate me. Reference then to something determinate, and some sort of adaptation to it worthy of the name of agreement, are thus constituent elements in the definition of any statement of mine as 'true.'

You cannot get at either the reference or the adaptation without using the notion of the workings. *That* the thing is, *what* it is, and *which* it is (of all the possible things with that

218

what) are points determinable only by the pragmatic method. The 'which' means a possibility of pointing, or of otherwise singling out the special object; the 'what' means choice on our part of an essential aspect to conceive it by (and this is always relative to what Dewey calls our own 'situation'); and the 'that' means our assumption of the attitude of belief, the reality-recognizing attitude. Surely for understanding what the word 'true' means as applied to a statement, the mention of such workings is indispensable. Surely if we leave them out the subject and the object of the cognitive relation float — in the same universe, 't is true — but vaguely and ignorantly and without mutual contact or mediation.

Our critics nevertheless call the workings inessential. No functional possibilities 'make' our beliefs true, they say; they are true inherently, true positively, born 'true' as the Count of Chambord was born 'Henri-Cinq.' Pragmatism insists, on the contrary, that statements and beliefs are thus inertly and statically true only by courtesy: they practically pass for true; but you *cannot define what you mean* by calling them true without referring to their functional possibilities. These give its whole *logical content* to that relation to reality on a belief's part to which the name 'truth' is applied, a relation which otherwise remains one of mere coexistence or bare withness.

The foregoing statements reproduce the essential content of the lecture on Truth in my book *Pragmatism*. Schiller's doctrine of 'humanism,' Dewey's 'Studies in logical theory,' and my own 'radical empiricism,' all involve this general notion of truth as 'working,' either actual or conceivable. But they envelop it as only one detail in the midst of much wider theories that aim eventually at determining the notion of what 'reality' at large is in its ultimate nature and constitution.

X

THE EXISTENCE OF JULIUS CÆSAR[1]

My account of truth is purely logical and relates to its definition only. I contend that you cannot tell what the *word* 'true' *means*, as applied to a statement, without invoking the *concept of the statement's workings.*

Assume, to fix our ideas, a universe composed of two things only: imperial Cæsar dead and turned to clay, and me, saying 'Cæsar really existed.' Most persons would naïvely deem truth to be thereby uttered, and say that by a sort of *actio in distans* my statement had taken direct hold of the other fact.

But have my words so certainly denoted *that* Cæsar? — or so certainly connoted *his* individual attributes? To fill out the complete measure of what the epithet 'true' may ideally mean, my thought ought to bear a fully determinate and unambiguous 'one-to-one-rela-

---

[1] Originally printed under the title of 'Truth versus Truthfulness,' in the *Journal of Philosophy.*

tion' to its own particular object. In the ultra-simple universe imagined the reference is un-certified. Were there two Cæsars we should n't know which was meant. The conditions of truth thus seem incomplete in this universe of discourse so that it must be enlarged.

Transcendentalists enlarge it by invoking an absolute mind which, as it owns all the facts, can sovereignly correlate them. If it intends that my statement *shall* refer to that identical Cæsar, and that the attributes I have in mind *shall* mean his attributes, that intention suf-fices to make the statement true.

I, in turn, enlarge the universe by admitting finite intermediaries between the two original facts. Cæsar *had*, and my statement *has*, ef-fects; and if these effects in any way run to-gether, a concrete medium and bottom is pro-vided for the determinate cognitive relation, which, as a pure *actio in distans*, seemed to float too vaguely and unintelligibly.

The real Cæsar, for example, wrote a man-uscript of which I see a real reprint, and say 'the Cæsar I mean is the author of *that*.' The workings of my thought thus determine both its denotative and its connotative significance more fully. It now defines itself as neither irrelevant to the real Cæsar, nor false in what it suggests of him. The absolute mind, seeing me thus working towards Cæsar through the cosmic intermediaries, might well say: 'Such workings only specify in detail what I meant myself by the statement being true. I decree the cognitive relation between the two original facts to mean that just that kind of concrete chain of intermediaries exists or can exist.'

But the chain involves facts prior to the statement the logical conditions of whose truth we are defining, and facts subsequent to it; and this circumstance, coupled with the vulgar employment of the terms truth and fact as synonyms, has laid my account open to misapprehension. 'How,' it is confusedly asked, 'can Cæsar's existence, a truth already 2000 years old, depend for its truth on anything about to happen now? How can my acknowledgment of it be made true by the acknowledgment's own effects? The effects may indeed confirm my belief, but the belief was made true already by the fact that Cæsar really did exist.'

Well, be it so, for if there were no Cæsar, there could, of course, be no positive truth about him — but then distinguish between 'true' as being positively and completely so established, and 'true' as being so only 'practically,' elliptically, and by courtesy, in the sense of not being positively irrelevant or *un*-true. Remember also that Cæsar's having existed in fact may make a present statement false or irrelevant as well as it may make it true, and that in neither case does it itself have to alter. It being given, whether truth, untruth, or irrelevancy shall be also given depends on something coming from the statement itself. What pragmatism contends for is that you cannot adequately *define* the something if you leave the notion of the statement's functional workings out of your account. Truth meaning agreement with reality, the mode of the agreeing is a practical problem which the subjective term of the relation alone can solve.

THE EXISTENCE OF CÆSAR

NOTE. This paper was originally followed by a couple of paragraphs meant to conciliate the intellectualist opposition. Since you love the word 'true' so, and since you despise so the concrete working of our ideas, I said, keep the word 'truth' for the saltatory and incomprehensible relation you care so much for, and I will say of thoughts that know their objects in an intelligible sense that they are 'truthful.'

Like most offerings, this one has been spurned, so I revoke it, repenting of my generosity. Professor Pratt, in his recent book, calls any objective state of *facts* 'a truth,' and uses the word 'trueness' in the sense of 'truth' as proposed by me. Mr. Hawtrey (see below, page 281) uses 'correctness' in the same sense. Apart from the general evil of ambiguous vocabularies, we may really forsake all hope, if the term 'truth' is officially to lose its status as a property of our beliefs and opinions, and become recognized as a technical synonym for 'fact.'

XI

THE ABSOLUTE AND THE STRENUOUS LIFE[1]

Professor W. A. Brown, in the *Journal* for August 15, approves my pragmatism for allowing that a belief in the absolute may give holidays to the spirit, but takes me to task for the narrowness of this concession, and shows by striking examples how great a power the same belief may have in letting loose the strenuous life.

I have no criticism whatever to make upon his excellent article, but let me explain why 'moral holidays' were the only gift of the absolute which I picked out for emphasis. I was primarily concerned in my lectures with contrasting the belief that the world is still in process of making with the belief that there is an 'eternal' edition of it ready-made and complete. The former, or 'pluralistic' belief, was the one that my pragmatism favored. Both

[1] Reprinted from the *Journal of Philosophy*, etc., 1906.

beliefs confirm our strenuous moods. Pluralism actually demands them, since it makes
the world's salvation depend upon the ener-
gizing of its several parts, among which we
are. Monism permits them, for however furi-
ous they may be, we can always justify ourselves in advance for indulging them by the
thought that they *will have been* expressions of
the absolute's perfect life. By escaping from
your finite perceptions to the conception of the
eternal whole, you can hallow any tendency
whatever. Tho the absolute *dictates* nothing,
it will *sanction* anything and everything after
the fact, for whatever is once there will
have to be regarded as an integral member of
the universe's perfection. Quietism and frenzy
thus alike receive the absolute's permit to
exist. Those of us who are naturally inert
may abide in our resigned passivity; those
whose energy is excessive may grow more reck-
less still. History shows how easily both quiet-
ists and fanatics have drawn inspiration from
the absolutistic scheme. It suits sick souls and
strenuous ones equally well.

One cannot say thus of pluralism. Its world is always vulnerable, for some part may go astray; and having no 'eternal' edition of it to draw comfort from, its partisans must always feel to some degree insecure. If, as pluralists, we grant ourselves moral holidays, they can only be provisional breathing-spells, intended to refresh us for the morrow's fight. This forms one permanent inferiority of pluralism from the pragmatic point of view. It has no saving message for incurably sick souls. Absolutism, among its other messages, has that message, and is the only scheme that has it necessarily. That constitutes its chief superiority and is the source of its religious power. That is why, desiring to do it full justice, I valued its aptitude for moral-holiday giving so highly. Its claims in that way are unique, whereas its affinities with strenuousness are less emphatic than those of the pluralistic scheme.

In the last lecture of my book I candidly admitted this inferiority of pluralism. It lacks the wide indifference that absolutism shows. It is bound to disappoint many sick souls whom absolutism can console. It seems therefore poor tactics for absolutists to make little of this advantage. The needs of sick souls are surely the most urgent; and believers in the absolute should rather hold it to be great merit in their philosophy that it can meet them so well.

The pragmatism or pluralism which I defend has to fall back on a certain ultimate hardihood, a certain willingness to live without assurances or guarantees. To minds thus willing to live on possibilities that are not certainties, quietistic religion, sure of salvation *any how*, has a slight flavor of fatty degeneration about it which has caused it to be looked askance on, even in the church. Which side is right here, who can say? Within religion, emotion is apt to be tyrannical; but philosophy must favor the emotion that allies itself best with the whole body and drift of all the truths in sight. I conceive this to be the more strenuous type of emotion; but I have to admit that its inability to let loose quietistic raptures is a serious deficiency in the pluralistic philosophy which I profess.

XII

PROFESSOR HÉBERT ON PRAGMATISM[1]

Professor Marcel Hébert is a singularly erudite and liberal thinker (a seceder, I believe, from the Catholic priesthood) and an uncommonly direct and clear writer. His book *Le Divin* is one of the ablest reviews of the general subject of religious philosophy which recent years have produced; and in the small volume the title of which is copied above he has, perhaps, taken more pains not to do injustice to pragmatism than any of its numerous critics. Yet the usual fatal misapprehension of its purposes vitiates his exposition and his critique. His pamphlet seems to me to form a worthy hook, as it were, on which to hang one more attempt to tell the reader what the pragmatist account of truth really means.

[1] Reprint from the *Journal of Philosophy* for December 3, 1908 (vol. v, p. 689), of a review of *Le pragmatisme et ses diverses formes anglo-américaines,* by Marcel Hébert. (Paris: Librairie critique Emile Nourry. 1908. Pp. 105.)

M. Hébert takes it to mean what most people take it to mean, the doctrine, namely, that whatever proves subjectively expedient in the way of our thinking is 'true' in the absolute and unrestricted sense of the word, whether it corresponds to any objective state of things outside of our thought or not. Assuming this to be the pragmatist thesis, M. Hébert opposes it at length. Thought that proves itself to be thus expedient may, indeed, have every *other* kind of value for the thinker, he says, but cognitive value, representative value, *valeur de connaissance proprement dite*, it has not; and when it does have a high degree of general utility value, this is in every case derived from its previous value in the way of correctly representing independent objects that have an important influence on our lives. Only by thus representing things truly do we reap the useful fruits. But the fruits follow on the truth, they do not constitute it; so M. Hébert accuses pragmatism of telling us everything about truth except what it essentially is. He admits, indeed, that the world is so framed that when men have true ideas of realities, consequential utilities ensue in abundance; and no one of our critics, I think, has shown as concrete a sense of the variety of these utilities as he has; but he reiterates that, whereas such utilities are secondary, we insist on treating them as primary, and that the *connaissance objective* from which they draw all their being is something which we neglect, exclude, and destroy. The utilitarian value and the strictly cognitive value of our ideas may perfectly well harmonize, he says — and in the main he allows that they do harmonize — but they are not logically identical for that. He admits that subjective interests, desires, impulses may even have the active 'primacy' in our intellectual life. Cognition awakens only at their spur, and follows their cues and aims; yet, when it *is* awakened, it is objective cognition proper and not merely another name for the impulsive tendencies themselves in the state of satisfaction. The owner of a picture ascribed to Corot gets uneasy when its authenticity is doubted. He looks up its origin and is reassured. But his

uneasiness does not make the proposition
false, any more than his relief makes the proposition true, that the actual Corot was the
painter. Pragmatism, which, according to
M. Hébert, claims that our sentiments *make*
truth and falsehood, would oblige us to conclude that our minds exert no genuinely cognitive function whatever.

This subjectivist interpretation of our position seems to follow from my having happened
to write (without supposing it necessary to
explain that I was treating of cognition solely
on its subjective side) that in the long run the
true is the expedient in the way of our thinking,
much as the good is the expedient in the way of
our behavior! Having previously written that
truth means 'agreement with reality,' and insisted that the chief part of the expediency of
any one opinion is its agreement with the rest
of acknowledged truth, I apprehended no
exclusively subjectivistic reading of my meaning. My mind was so filled with the notion of
objective reference that I never dreamed that
my hearers would let go of it; and the very last

accusation I expected was that in speaking of
ideas and their satisfactions, I was denying
realities outside. My only wonder now is that
critics should have found so silly a personage
as I must have seemed in their eyes, worthy of
explicit refutation.

The object, for me, is just as much one part
of reality as the idea is another part. The truth
of the idea is one relation of it to the reality,
just as its date and its place are other relations.
All three relations *consist* of intervening parts
of the universe which can in every particular
case be assigned and catalogued, and which
differ in every instance of truth, just as they
differ with every date and place.

The pragmatist thesis, as Dr. Schiller and I
hold it, — I prefer to let Professor Dewey speak
for himself, — is that the relation called 'truth'
is thus concretely *definable*. Ours is the only
articulate attempt in the field to say positively
what truth actually *consists of*. Our de-
nouncers have literally nothing to oppose to it
as an alternative. For them, when an idea is
true, it *is* true, and there the matter terminates,

the word 'true' being indefinable. The relation of the true idea to its object, being, as they think, unique, it can be expressed in terms of nothing else, and needs only to be named for any one to recognize and understand it. Moreover it is invariable and universal, the same in every single instance of truth, however diverse the ideas, the realities, and the other relations between them may be.

Our pragmatist view, on the contrary, is that the truth-relation is a definitely experienceable relation, and therefore describable as well as namable; that it is not unique in kind, and neither invariable nor universal. The relation to its object that makes an idea true in any given instance, is, we say, embodied in intermediate details of reality which lead towards the object, which vary in every instance, and which in every instance can be concretely traced. The chain of workings which an opinion sets up *is* the opinion's truth, falsehood, or irrelevancy, as the case may be. Every idea that a man has works some consequences in him, in the shape either of bodily

actions or of other ideas. Through these consequences the man's relations to surrounding
realities are modified. He is carried nearer to
some of them and farther from others, and
gets now the feeling that the idea has worked
satisfactorily, now that it has not. The idea
has put him into touch with something that
fulfils its intent, or it has not.

This something is the *man's object*, primarily. Since the only realities we can talk
about are such *objects-believed-in*, the pragmatist, whenever he says 'reality,' means in the
first instance what may count for the man himself as a reality, what he believes at the moment to be such. Sometimes the reality is a
concrete sensible presence. The idea, for example, may be that a certain door opens into a
room where a glass of beer may be bought. If
opening the door leads to the actual sight and
taste of the beer, the man calls the idea true.
Or his idea may be that of an abstract relation,
say of that between the sides and the hypothe-
nuse of a triangle, such a relation being, of
course, a reality quite as much as a glass of

beer is. If the thought of such a relation leads him to draw auxiliary lines and to compare the figures they make, he may at last, perceiving one equality after another, *see* the relation thought of, by a vision quite as particular and direct as was the taste of the beer. If he does so, he calls *that* idea, also, true. His idea has, in each case, brought him into closer touch with a reality felt at the moment to verify just that idea. Each reality verifies and validates its own idea exclusively; and in each case the verification consists in the satisfactorily-ending consequences, mental or physical, which the idea was able to set up. These 'workings' differ in every single instance, they never transcend experience, they consist of particulars, mental or sensible, and they admit of concrete description in every individual case. Pragmatists are unable to see what you can possibly *mean* by calling an idea true, unless you mean that between it as a *terminus a quo* in some one's mind and some particular reality as a *terminus ad quem*, such concrete workings do or may intervene. Their direction constitutes the idea's reference to that reality, their satisfactoriness constitutes its adaptation thereto, and the two things together constitute the 'truth' of the idea for its possessor. Without such intermediating portions of concretely real experience the pragmatist sees no materials out of which the adaptive relation called truth can be built up.

The anti-pragmatist view is that the workings are but evidences of the truth's previous inherent presence in the idea, and that you can wipe the very possibility of them out of existence and still leave the truth of the idea as solid as ever. But surely this is not a counter-theory of truth to ours. It is the renunciation of all articulate theory. It is but a claim to the right to call certain ideas true anyhow; and this is what I meant above by saying that the anti-pragmatists offer us no real alternative, and that our account is literally the only positive theory extant. What meaning, indeed, can an idea's truth have save its power of adapting us either mentally or physically to a reality?

How comes it, then, that our critics so uniformly accuse us of subjectivism, of denying the reality's existence? It comes, I think, from the necessary predominance of subjective language in our analysis. However independent and ejective realities may be, we can talk about them, in framing our accounts of truth, only as so many objects believed-in. But the process of experience leads men so continually to supersede their older objects by newer ones which they find it more satisfactory to believe in, that the notion of an *absolute* reality inevitably arises as a *grenzbegriff*, equivalent to that of an object that shall never be superseded, and belief in which shall be *endgültig*. Cognitively we thus live under a sort of rule of three: as our private concepts represent the sense-objects to which they lead us, these being public realities independent of the individual, so these sense-realities may, in turn, represent realities of a hypersensible order, electrons, mind-stuff, God, or what not, existing independently of all human thinkers. The notion of such final realities, knowledge of which would be absolute truth, is an outgrowth of our

cognitive experience from which neither pragmatists nor anti-pragmatists escape. They
form an inevitable regulative postulate in every
one's thinking. Our notion of them is the most
abundantly suggested and satisfied of all our
beliefs, the last to suffer doubt. The difference
is that our critics use this belief as their sole par-
adigm, and treat any one who talks of human realities as if he thought the notion of reality 'in
itself' illegitimate. Meanwhile, reality-in-itself,
so far as by them *talked of*, is only a human object; they postulate it just as we postulate it; and
if we are subjectivists they are so no less. Realities in themselves can be there *for* any one,
whether pragmatist or anti-pragmatist, only
by being believed; they are believed only by
their notions appearing true; and their notions
appear true only because they work satisfactorily. Satisfactorily, moreover, for the particular thinker's purpose. There is no idea
which is *the* true idea, of anything. Whose is
the true idea of the absolute? Or to take
M. Hébert's example, what is *the* true idea of a
picture which you possess? It is the idea that

most satisfactorily meets your present interest. The interest may be in the picture's place, its age, its 'tone,' its subject, its dimensions, its authorship, its price, its merit, or what not. If its authorship by Corot have been doubted, what will satisfy the interest aroused in you at that moment will be to have your claim to own a Corot confirmed; but, if you have a normal human mind, merely calling it a Corot will not satisfy other demands of your mind at the same time. For *them* to be satisfied, what you learn of the picture must make smooth connection with what you know of the rest of the system of reality in which the actual Corot played his part. M. Hébert accuses us of holding that the proprietary satisfactions of themselves suffice to make the belief true, and that, so far as we are concerned, no actual Corot need ever have existed. Why we should be thus cut off from the more general and intellectual satisfactions, I know not; but whatever the satisfactions may be, intellectual or proprietary, they belong to the subjective side of the truth-relation. They found our beliefs; our beliefs are in realities;

if no realities are there, the beliefs are false; but if realities are there, how they can ever be *known* without first being *believed;* or how *believed* except by our first having ideas of them that work satisfactorily, pragmatists find it impossible to imagine. They also find it impossible to imagine what makes the anti-pragmatists' dogmatic 'ipse dixit' assurance of reality more credible than the pragmatists' conviction based on concrete verifications. M. Hébert will probably agree to this, when put in this way, so I do not see our inferiority to him in the matter of *connaissance propre-ment dite.*

Some readers will say that, altho *I* may possibly believe in realities beyond our ideas, Dr. Schiller, at any rate, does not. This is a great misunderstanding, for Schiller's doctrine and mine are identical, only our expositions follow different directions. He starts from the subjective pole of the chain, the individual with his beliefs, as the more concrete and immediately given phenomenon. 'An individual claims his belief to be true,' Schiller says, 'but what does he mean by true? and how does he establish the claim?' With these questions we embark on a psychological inquiry. To be true, it appears, means, *for that individual*, to work satisfactorily for him; and the working and the satisfaction, since they vary from case to case, admit of no universal description. What works is true and represents a reality, for the individual for whom it works. If he is infallible, the reality is 'really' there; if mistaken it is not there, or not there as he thinks it. We all believe, when our ideas work satisfactorily; but we don't yet know who of us is infallible; so that the problem of truth and that of error are *ebenbürtig* and arise out of the same situations. Schiller, remaining with the fallible individual, and treating only of reality-for-him, seems to many of his readers to ignore reality-in-itself altogether. But that is because he seeks only to tell us how truths are attained, not what the content of those truths, when attained, shall be. It may be that the truest of all beliefs shall be that in transsubjective realities. It certainly *seems* the truest, for no rival belief is as voluminously satisfactory, and it is probably Dr. Schiller's own belief; but he is not required, for his immediate purpose, to profess it. Still less is he obliged to assume it in advance as the basis of his discussion.

I, however, warned by the ways of critics, adopt different tactics. I start from the object-pole of the idea-reality chain and follow it in the opposite direction from Schiller's. Anticipating the results of the general truth-processes of mankind, I begin with the abstract notion of an objective reality. I postulate it, and ask on my own account, *I vouching for this reality,* what would make any one else's idea of it true for me as well as for him. But I find no different answer from that which Schiller gives. If the other man's idea leads him, not only to believe that the reality is there, but to use it as the reality's temporary substitute, by letting it evoke adaptive thoughts and acts similar to those which the reality itself would provoke, then it is true in the only intelligible sense, true through its particular consequences, and true for me as well as for the man.

My account is more of a logical definition; Schiller's is more of a psychological description. Both treat an absolutely identical matter of experience, only they traverse it in opposite ways.

Possibly these explanations may satisfy M. Hébert, whose little book, apart from the false accusation of subjectivism, gives a fairly instructive account of the pragmatist epistemology.

XIII

ABSTRACTIONISM AND 'RELATIVISMUS'

Abstract concepts, such as elasticity, voluminousness, disconnectedness, are salient aspects of our concrete experiences which we find it useful to single out. Useful, because we are then reminded of other things that offer those same aspects; and, if the aspects carry consequences in those other things, we can return to our first things, expecting those same consequences to accrue.

To be helped to anticipate consequences is always a gain, and such being the help that abstract concepts give us, it is obvious that their use is fulfilled only when we get back again into concrete particulars by their means, bearing the consequences in our minds, and enriching our notion of the original objects therewithal.

Without abstract concepts to handle our perceptual particulars by, we are like men hopping on one foot. Using concepts along with the particulars, we become bipedal. We throw our concept forward, get a foothold on the consequence, hitch our line to this, and draw our percept up, travelling thus with a hop, skip and jump over the surface of life at a vastly rapider rate than if we merely waded through the thickness of the particulars as accident rained them down upon our heads. Animals have to do this, but men raise their heads higher and breathe freely in the upper conceptual air.

The enormous esteem professed by all philosophers for the conceptual form of consciousness is easy to understand. From Plato's time downwards it has been held to be our sole avenue to essential truth. Concepts are universal, changeless, pure; their relations are eternal; they are spiritual, while the concrete particulars which they enable us to handle are corrupted by the flesh. They are precious in themselves, then, apart from their original use, and confer new dignity upon our life.

One can find no fault with this way of feeling about concepts so long as their original function does not get swallowed up in the admiration and lost. That function is of course to enlarge mentally our momentary experiences by *adding* to them the consequences conceived; but unfortunately, that function is not only too often forgotten by philosophers in their reasonings, but is often converted into its exact opposite, and made a means of diminishing the original experience by *denying* (implicitly or explicitly) all its features save the one specially abstracted to conceive it by.

This itself is a highly abstract way of stating my complaint, and it needs to be redeemed from obscurity by showing instances of what is meant. Some beliefs very dear to my own heart have been conceived in this viciously abstract way by critics. One is the 'will to believe,' so called; another is the indeterminism of certain futures; a third is the notion that truth may vary with the standpoint of the man who holds it. I believe that the perverse abuse of the abstracting function has led critics to employ false arguments against these doctrines, and often has led their readers too to false conclusions. I should like to try to save the situation, if possible, by a few counter-critical remarks.

Let me give the name of 'vicious abstractionism' to a way of using concepts which may be thus described: We conceive a concrete situation by singling out some salient or important feature in it, and classing it under that; then, instead of adding to its previous characters all the positive consequences which the new way of conceiving it may bring, we proceed to use our concept privatively; reducing the originally rich phenomenon to the naked suggestions of that name abstractly taken, treating it as a case of 'nothing but' that concept, and acting as if all the other characters from out of which the concept is abstracted were expunged.[1] Abstraction, functioning in this way, becomes a means of arrest far more than a means of advance in thought. It mutilates things; it creates difficulties and finds impossi-

[1] Let not the reader confound the fallacy here described with legitimately negative inferences such as those drawn in the mood 'celarent' of the logic-books.

bilities; and more than half the trouble that metaphysicians and logicians give themselves over the paradoxes and dialectic puzzles of the universe may, I am convinced, be traced to this relatively simple source. *The viciously privative employment of abstract characters and class names* is, I am persuaded, one of the great original sins of the rationalistic mind.

To proceed immediately to concrete examples, cast a glance at the belief in 'free will,' demolished with such specious persuasiveness recently by the skilful hand of Professor Fullerton.[1] When a common man says that his will is free, what does he mean? He means that there are situations of bifurcation inside of his life in which two futures seem to him equally possible, for both have their roots equally planted in his present and his past. Either, if realized, will grow out of his previous motives, character and circumstances, and will continue uninterruptedly the pulsations of his personal life. But sometimes both at once are incom-

[1] *Popular Science Monthly*, N. Y., vols. lviii and lix.

patible with physical nature, and then it seems to the naïve observer as if he made a choice between them *now*, and that the question of which future is to be, instead of having been decided at the foundation of the world, were decided afresh at every passing moment in which fact seems livingly to grow, and possibility seems, in turning itself towards one act, to exclude all others.

He who takes things at their face-value here may indeed be deceived. He may far too often mistake his private ignorance of what is predetermined for a real indetermination of what is to be. Yet, however imaginary it may be, his picture of the situation offers no appearance of breach between the past and future. A train is the same train, its passengers are the same passengers, its momentum is the same momentum, no matter which way the switch which fixes its direction is placed. For the indeterminist there is at all times enough past for all the different futures in sight, and more besides, to find their reasons in it, and whichever future comes will slide out of that past as easily as the train slides by the switch. The world, in short, is just as *continuous with itself* for the believers in free will as for the rigorous determinists, only the latter are unable to believe in points of bifurcation as spots of really indifferent equilibrium or as containing shunts which there — and there only, *not before* — direct existing motions without altering their amount.

Were there such spots of indifference, the rigorous determinists think, the future and the past would be separated absolutely, for, *abstractly taken, the word 'indifferent' suggests disconnection solely.* Whatever is indifferent is in so far forth unrelated and detached. Take the term thus strictly, and you see, they tell us, that if any spot of indifference is found upon the broad highway between the past and the future, then *no* connection of any sort whatever, no continuous momentum, no identical passenger, no common aim or agent, can be found on both sides of the shunt or switch which there is moved. The place is an impassable chasm.

ABSTRACTIONISM

Mr. Fullerton writes — the italics are mine
— as follows : —

'In so far as my action is free, what I have
been, what I am, what I have always done or
striven to do, what I most earnestly wish or
resolve to do at the present moment — these
things can have *no more to do with its future
realization than if they had no existence.* . . .
The possibility is a hideous one; and surely
even the most ardent free-willist will, when
he contemplates it frankly, excuse me for hop-
ing that if I am free I am at least not very free,
and that I may reasonably expect to find *some*
degree of consistency in my life and actions.
. . . Suppose that I have given a dollar to a
blind beggar. Can *I*, if it is really an act of
free-will, be properly said to have given the
money ? Was it given because I was a man
of tender heart, etc., etc. ? . . . What has all
this to do with acts of free-will ? If they are
free, they must not be conditioned by antecedent circumstances of *any* sort, by the misery
of the beggar, by the pity in the heart of the
passer-by. They must be causeless, not deter-

mined. They must drop from a clear sky out of the void, for just in so far as they can be accounted for, they are not free.'[1]

Heaven forbid that I should get entangled here in a controversy about the rights and wrongs of the free-will question at large, for I am only trying to illustrate vicious abstractionism by the conduct of some of the doctrine's assailants. The moments of bifurcation, as the indeterminist seems to himself to experience them, are moments both of re-direction and of continuation. But because in the 'either — or' of the re-direction we hesitate, the determinist abstracts this little element of discontinuity from the superabundant continuities of the experience, and cancels in its behalf all the connective characters with which the latter is filled. Choice, for him, means henceforward *dis*connection pure and simple, something undetermined in advance *in any respect whatever*, and a life of choices must be a raving chaos, at no two moments of which could we be treated as one and the

[1] *Loc. cit.*, vol. lviii, pp. 189, 188.

same man. If Nero were 'free' at the moment of ordering his mother's murder, Mr. McTaggart[1] assures us that no one would have the right at any other moment to call him a bad man, for he would then be an absolutely other Nero.

A polemic author ought not merely to destroy his victim. He ought to try a bit to make him feel his error — perhaps not enough to convert him, but enough to give him a bad conscience and to weaken the energy of his defence. These violent caricatures of men's beliefs arouse only contempt for the incapacity of their authors to see the situations out of which the problems grow. To treat the negative character of one abstracted element as annulling all the positive features with which it coexists, is no way to change any actual indeterminist's way of looking on the matter, tho it may make the gallery applaud.

Turn now to some criticisms of the 'will to believe,' as another example of the vicious way

---

[1] *Some Dogmas of Religion*, p. 179.

in which abstraction is currently employed.
The right to believe in things for the truth of
which complete objective proof is yet lacking
is defended by those who apprehend certain
human situations in their concreteness. In
those situations the mind has alternatives before it so vast that the full evidence for either
branch is missing, and yet so significant that
simply to wait for proof, and to doubt while
waiting, might often in practical respects be
the same thing as weighing down the negative
side. Is life worth while at all? Is there any
general meaning in all this cosmic weather?
Is anything being permanently bought by all
this suffering? Is there perhaps a transmun-
dane experience in Being, something corresponding to a 'fourth dimension,' which, if we
had access to it, might patch up some of this
world's *zerrissenheit* and make things look
more rational than they at first appear? Is
there a superhuman consciousness of which
our minds are parts, and from which inspiration and help may come? Such are the questions in which the right to take sides practi-

cally for yes or no is affirmed by some of us, while others hold that this is methodologically inadmissible, and summon us to die professing ignorance and proclaiming the duty of every one to refuse to believe.

I say nothing of the personal inconsistency of some of these critics, whose printed works furnish exquisite illustrations of the will to believe, in spite of their denunciations of it as a phrase and as a recommended thing. Mr. McTaggart, whom I will once more take as an example, is sure that 'reality is rational and righteous' and 'destined *sub specie temporis* to become perfectly good'; and his calling this belief a result of necessary logic has surely never deceived any reader as to its real genesis in the gifted author's mind. Mankind is made on too uniform a pattern for any of us to escape successfully from acts of faith. We have a lively vision of what a certain view of the universe would mean for us. We kindle or we shudder at the thought, and our feeling runs through our whole logical nature and animates its workings. It *can't* be that, we feel; it *must* be this. It must be what it *ought* to be, and it *ought* to be this; and then we seek for every reason, good or bad, to make this which so deeply ought to be, seem objectively the probable thing. We show the arguments against it to be insufficient, so that it *may* be true; we represent its appeal to be to our whole nature's loyalty and not to any emaciated faculty of syllogistic proof. We reinforce it by remembering the enlargement of our world by music, by thinking of the promises of sunsets and the impulses from vernal woods. And the essence of the whole experience, when the individual swept through it says finally 'I believe,' is the intense concreteness of his vision, the individuality of the hypothesis before him, and the complexity of the various concrete motives and perceptions that issue in his final state.

But see now how the abstractionist treats this rich and intricate vision that a certain state of things must be true. He accuses the believer of reasoning by the following syllogism: —

All good desires must be fulfilled;

The desire to believe this proposition is a good desire;

Ergo, this proposition must be believed.

He substitutes this abstraction for the concrete state of mind of the believer, pins the naked absurdity of it upon him, and easily proves that any one who defends him must be the greatest fool on earth. As if any real believer ever thought in this preposterous way, or as if any defender of the legitimacy of men's concrete ways of concluding ever used the abstract and general premise, 'All desires must be fulfilled'! Nevertheless, Mr. McTaggart solemnly and laboriously refutes the syllogism in sections 47 to 57 of the above-cited book. He shows that there is no fixed link in the dictionary between the abstract concepts 'desire,' 'goodness' and 'reality'; and he ignores all the links which in the single concrete case the believer feels and perceives to be there! He adds : —

'When the reality of a thing is uncertain, the argument encourages us to suppose that our approval of a thing can determine its reality.

And when this unhallowed link has once been established, retribution overtakes us. For when the reality of the thing is independently certain, we [then] have to admit that the reality of the thing should determine our approval of that thing. I find it difficult to imagine a more degraded position.'

One here feels tempted to quote ironically Hegel's famous equation of the real with the rational to his english disciple, who ends his chapter with the heroic words : —

'For those who do not pray, there remains the resolve that, so far as their strength may permit, neither the pains of death nor the pains of life shall drive them to any comfort in that which they hold to be false, or drive them from any comfort [discomfort?] in that which they hold to be true.'

How can so ingenious-minded a writer fail to see how far over the heads of the enemy all his arrows pass? When Mr. McTaggart himself believes that the universe is run by the dialectic energy of the absolute idea, his insistent desire to have a world of that sort is felt by him to be no chance example of desire in general, but an altogether peculiar *insight-giving passion* to which, in this if in no other instance, he would be *stupid* not to yield. He obeys its concrete singularity, not the bare abstract feature in it of being a 'desire.' His situation is as particular as that of an actress who resolves that it is best for her to marry and leave the stage, of a priest who becomes secular, of a politician who abandons public life. What sensible man would seek to refute the concrete decisions of such persons by tracing them to abstract premises, such as that 'all actresses must marry,' 'all clergymen must be laymen,' 'all politicians should resign their posts'? Yet this type of refutation, absolutely unavailing though it be for purposes of conversion, is spread by Mr. McTaggart through many pages of his book. For the aboundingness of our real reasons he substitutes one narrow point. For men's real probabilities he gives a skeletonized abstraction which no man was ever tempted to believe.

The abstraction in my next example is less

simple, but is quite as flimsy as a weapon of attack. Empiricists think that truth in general is distilled from single men's beliefs; and the so-called pragmatists 'go them one better' by trying to define what it consists in when it comes. It consists, I have elsewhere said, in such a working on the part of the beliefs as may bring the man into satisfactory relations with objects to which these latter point. The working is of course a concrete working in the actual experience of human beings, among their ideas, feelings, perceptions, beliefs and acts, as well as among the physical things of their environment, and the relations must be understood as being possible as well as actual. In the chapter on truth of my book *Pragmatism* I have taken pains to defend energetically this view. Strange indeed have been the misconceptions of it by its enemies, and many have these latter been. Among the most formidable-sounding onslaughts on the attempt to introduce some concreteness into our notion of what the truth of an idea may mean, is one that has been raised in many quarters to the effect that to make truth grow in any way out of human opinion is but to reproduce that protagorean doctrine that the individual man is 'the measure of all things,' which Plato in his immortal dialogue, the Thæatetus, is unanimously said to have laid away so comfortably in its grave two thousand years ago. The two cleverest brandishers of this objection to make truth concrete, Professors Rickert and Münsterberg, write in German,[1] and 'relativismus' is the name they give to the heresy which they endeavor to uproot.

The first step in their campaign against 'relativismus' is entirely in the air. They accuse relativists — and we pragmatists are typical relativists — of being debarred by their self-adopted principles, not only from the privilege which rationalist philosophers enjoy, of believing that these principles of their own are truth impersonal and absolute, but even of framing the abstract notion of such a truth, *in the pragmatic sense, of an ideal opinion in*

[1] Münsterberg's book has just appeared in an english version: *The Eternal Values*, Boston, 1909.

which all men might agree, and which no man should ever wish to change. Both charges fall wide of their mark. I myself, as a pragmatist, believe in my own account of truth as firmly as any rationalist can possibly believe in his. And I believe in it for the very reason that I *have* the idea of truth which my learned adversaries contend that no pragmatist can frame. I expect, namely, that the more fully men discuss and test my account, the more they will agree that it *fits*, and the less will they desire a change. I may of course be premature in this confidence, and the glory of being truth final and absolute may fall upon some later revision and correction of my scheme, which latter will then be judged untrue in just the measure in which it departs from that finally satisfactory formulation. To admit, as we pragmatists do, that we are liable to correction (even tho we may not expect it) *involves* the use on our part of an ideal standard. Rationalists themselves are, as individuals, sometimes sceptical enough to admit the abstract possibility of their own present opinions being corrigible and

revisable to some degree, so the fact that
the mere *notion* of an absolute standard should
seem to them so important a thing to claim for
themselves and to deny to us is not easy to
explain. If, along with the notion of the standard, they could also claim its exclusive warrant for their own fulminations now, it would
be important to them indeed. But absolutists
like Rickert freely admit the sterility of the
notion, even in their own hands. Truth is
what we *ought* to believe, they say, even tho
no man ever did or shall believe it, and even
tho we have no way of getting at it save by
the usual empirical processes of testing our
opinions by one another and by facts. Pragmatically, then, this part of the dispute is idle.
No relativist who ever actually walked the
earth[1] has denied the regulative character in
his own thinking of the notion of absolute

[1] Of course the bugaboo creature called 'the sceptic' in the
logic-books, who dogmatically makes the statement that no
statement, not even the one he now makes, is true, is a mere
mechanical toy-target for the rationalist shooting-gallery —
hit him and he turns a summersault — yet he is the only sort
of relativist whom my colleagues appear able to imagine to
exist.

truth. What is challenged by relativists is the
pretence on any one's part to have found for
certain at any given moment what the shape
of that truth is. Since the better absolutists
agree in this, admitting that the proposition
'There *is* absolute truth' is the only absolute
truth of which we can be sure,[1] further debate is practically unimportant, so we may
pass to their next charge.

It is in this charge that the vicious abstractionism becomes most apparent. The anti-
pragmatist, in postulating absolute truth, refuses to give any account of what the words
may mean. For him they form a self-explana-
tory term. The pragmatist, on the contrary,
articulately defines their meaning. Truth ab-

---

[1] Compare Rickert's *Gegenstand der Erkentniss*, pp. 137,
138. Münsterberg's version of this first truth is that 'Es gibt
eine Welt,' — see his *Philosophie der Werte*, pp. 38 and 74
And, after all, both these philosophers confess in the end that
the primal truth of which they consider our supposed denial
so irrational is not properly an insight at all, but a dogma
adopted by the will which any one who turns his back on duty
may disregard! But if it all reverts to 'the will to believe,'
pragmatists have that privilege as well as their critics.

solute, he says, means an ideal set of formulations towards which all opinions may in the long run of experience be expected to converge. In this definition of absolute truth he not only postulates that there is a tendency to such convergence of opinions, to such ultimate consensus, but he postulates the other factors of his definition equally, borrowing them by anticipation from the true conclusions expected to be reached. He postulates the existence of opinions, he postulates the experience that will sift them, and the consistency which that experience will show. He justifies himself in these assumptions by saying that they are not postulates in the strict sense but simple inductions from the past extended to the future by analogy; and he insists that human opinion has already reached a pretty stable equilibrium regarding them, and that if its future development fails to alter them, the definition itself, with all its terms included, will be part of the very absolute truth which it defines. The hypothesis will, in short, have worked successfully all round the circle and proved self-corroborative, and the circle will be closed.

The anti-pragmatist, however, immediately falls foul of the word 'opinion' here, abstracts it from the universe of life, and uses it as a bare dictionary-substantive, to deny the rest of the assumptions which it coexists withal. The dictionary says that an opinion is 'what some one thinks or believes.' This definition leaves every one's opinion free to be autogenous, or unrelated either to what any one else may think or to what the truth may be. Therefore, continue our abstractionists, we must conceive it *as essentially thus unrelated*, so that even were a billion men to sport the same opinion, and only one man to differ, we could admit no collateral circumstances which might presumptively make it more probable that he, not they, should be wrong. Truth, they say, follows not the counting of noses, nor is it only another name for a majority vote. It is a relation that antedates experience, between our opinions and an independent something which the pragmatist account ignores, a relation which, tho the opinions of individuals should to all eternity deny it, would still remain to qualify them as false. To talk of opinions without referring to this independent something, the anti-pragmatist assures us, is to play Hamlet with Hamlet's part left out.

But when the pragmatist speaks of opinions, does he mean any such insulated and unmotived abstractions as are here supposed? Of course not, he means men's opinions in the flesh, as they have really formed themselves, opinions surrounded by their causes and the influences they obey and exert, and along with the whole environment of social communication of which they are a part and out of which they take their rise. Moreover the 'experience' which the pragmatic definition postulates *is* the independent something which the anti-pragmatist accuses him of ignoring. Already have men grown unanimous in the opinion that such experience is 'of' an independent reality, the existence of which all opinions must acknowledge, in order to be true. Already do they agree that in the long run it is useless to

resist experience's pressure; that the more of it
a man has, the better position he stands in, in
respect of truth; that some men, having had
more experience, are therefore better authori-
ties than others; that some are also wiser by
nature and better able to interpret the experience they have had; that it is one part of such
wisdom to compare notes, discuss, and follow the opinion of our betters; and that the
more systematically and thoroughly such comparison and weighing of opinions is pursued,
the truer the opinions that survive are likely to
be. *When the pragmatist talks of opinions, it
is opinions as they thus concretely and livingly
and interactingly and correlatively exist that
he has in mind;* and when the anti-pragmatist
tries to floor him because the word 'opinion'
can also be taken abstractly and as if it had
no environment, he simply ignores the soil out
of which the whole discussion grows. His
weapons cut the air and strike no blow. No one
gets wounded in the war against caricatures
of belief and skeletons of opinion of which the
German onslaughts upon 'relativismus' con-

sists. Refuse to use the word 'opinion' abstractly, keep it in its real environment, and the withers of pragmatism remain unwrung.

That men do exist who are 'opinionated,' in the sense that their opinions are self-willed, is unfortunately a fact that must be admitted, no matter what one's notion of truth in general may be. But that this fact should make it impossible for truth to form itself authentically out of the life of opinion is what no critic has yet proved. Truth may well consist of certain opinions, and does indeed consist of nothing but opinions, tho not every opinion need be true. No pragmatist needs to *dogmatize* about the consensus of opinion in the future being right — he need only *postulate* that it will probably contain more of truth than any one's opinion now.

XIV

TWO ENGLISH CRITICS

Mr. Bertrand Russell's article entitled 'Transatlantic Truth,'[1] has all the clearness, dialectic subtlety, and wit which one expects from his pen, but it entirely fails to hit the right point of view for apprehending our position. When, for instance, we say that a true proposition is one the consequences of believing which are good, he assumes us to mean that any one who believes a proposition to be true must first have made out clearly that its consequences *are* good, and that his belief must primarily be in that fact, — an obvious absurdity, for that fact is the deliverance of a new proposition, quite different from the first one and is, moreover, a fact usually very hard to verify, it being 'far easier,' as Mr. Russell justly says, 'to settle the plain question of fact: "Have popes always been infallible?" than to settle the question whether the effects

[1] In the *Albany Review* for January, 1908.

of thinking them infallible are on the whole good.'

We affirm nothing as silly as Mr. Russell supposes. Good consequences are not proposed by us merely as a sure sign, mark, or criterion, by which truth's presence is habitually ascertained, tho they may indeed serve on occasion as such a sign; they are proposed rather as the lurking *motive* inside of every truth-claim, whether the 'trower' be conscious of such motive, or whether he obey it blindly. They are proposed as the *causa existendi* of our beliefs, not as their logical cue or premise, and still less as their objective deliverance or content. They assign the only intelligible practical *meaning* to that difference in our beliefs which our habit of calling them true or false comports.

No truth-claimer except the pragmatist himself need ever be aware of the part played in his own mind by consequences, and he himself is aware of it only abstractly and in general, and may at any moment be quite oblivious of it with respect to his own beliefs.

Mr. Russell next joins the army of those

who inform their readers that according to the pragmatist definition of the word 'truth' the belief that A exists may be 'true,' even when A does *not* exist. This is the usual slander, repeated to satiety by our critics. They forget that in any concrete account of what is denoted by 'truth' in human life, the word can only be used relatively to some particular trower. Thus, I may hold it true that Shakespere wrote the plays that bear his name, and may express my opinion to a critic. If the critic be both a pragmatist and a baconian, he will in his capacity of pragmatist see plainly that the workings of my opinion, I being what I am, make it perfectly true for me, while in his capacity of baconian he still believes that Shakespere never wrote the plays in question. But most anti-pragmatist critics take the word 'truth' as something absolute, and easily play on their reader's readiness to treat his own truths as the absolute ones. If the reader whom they address believes that A does not exist, while we pragmatists show that those for whom the belief that it exists works satisfactorily will al-

ways call it true, he easily sneers at the naïveté
of our contention, for is not then the belief in
question 'true,' tho what it declares as fact
has, as the reader so well knows, no existence?
Mr. Russell speaks of our statement as an 'attempt to get rid of fact' and naturally enough
considers it 'a failure' (p. 410). 'The old notion
of truth reappears,' he adds — that notion being,
of course, that when a belief is true, its object
does exist.

It is, of course, *bound* to exist, on sound
pragmatic principles. Concepts signify consequences. How is the world made different
for me by my conceiving an opinion of mine
under the concept 'true'? First, an object
must be findable there (or sure signs of such
an object must be found) which shall agree
with the opinion. Second, such an opinion
must not be contradicted by anything else I
am aware of. But in spite of the obvious pragmatist requirement that when I have said truly
that something exists, it *shall* exist, the slander
which Mr. Russell repeats has gained the
widest currency.

Mr. Russell himself is far too witty and athletic a ratiocinator simply to repeat the slander dogmatically. Being nothing if not mathematical and logical, he must prove the accusation *secundum artem*, and convict us not so much of error as of absurdity. I have sincerely tried to follow the windings of his mind in this procedure, but for the life of me I can only see in it another example of what I have called (above, p. 249) vicious abstractionism. The abstract world of mathematics and pure logic is so native to Mr. Russell that he thinks that we describers of the functions of concrete fact must also mean fixed mathematical terms and functions. A mathematical term, as a, b, c, x, y, sin., log., is self-sufficient, and terms of this sort, once equated, can be substituted for one another in endless series without error. Mr. Russell, and also Mr. Hawtrey, of whom I shall speak presently, seem to think that in our mouth also such terms as 'meaning,' 'truth,' 'belief,' 'object,' 'definition,' are self-sufficients with no context of varying relation that might be further asked about. What a word means is expressed by its definition, is n't it? The definition claims to be exact and adequate, does n't it? Then it can be substituted for the word — since the two are identical — can't it? Then two words with the same definition can be substituted for one another, n'est-ce pas? Likewise two definitions of the same word, *nicht wahr*, etc., etc., till it will be indeed strange if you can't convict some one of self-contradiction and absurdity.

The particular application of this rigoristic treatment to my own little account of truth as working seems to be something like what follows. I say 'working' is what the 'truth' of our ideas means, and call it a definition. But since meanings and things meant, definitions and things defined, are equivalent and interchangeable, and nothing extraneous to its definition can be meant when a term is used, it follows that whoso calls an idea true, and means by that word that it works, cannot mean anything else, can believe nothing but that it does work, and in particular can neither imply nor allow anything about its object or deliverance. 'According to the pragmatists,' Mr. Russell writes, 'to say "it is true that other people exist" means "it is useful to believe that other people exist." But if so, then these two phrases are merely different words for the same proposition; therefore when I believe the one I believe the other' (p. 400). [Logic, I may say in passing, would seem to require Mr. Russell to believe them both at once, but he ignores this consequence, and considers that 'other people exist' and 'it is useful to believe that they do *even if they don't*,' must be identical and therefore substitutable propositions in the pragmatist mouth.]

But may not real terms, I now ask, have accidents not expressed in their definitions? and when a real value is finally substituted for the result of an algebraic series of substituted definitions, do not all these accidents creep back? Beliefs have their objective 'content' or 'deliverance' as well as their truth, and truth has its implications as well as its workings. If any one believe that other men exist,

it is both a content of his belief and an implication of its truth, that they should exist in
fact. Mr. Russell's logic would seem to exclude, 'by definition,' all such accidents as
contents, implications, and associates, and
would represent us as translating all belief into
a sort of belief in pragmatism itself — of all
things! If I say that a speech is eloquent, and
explain 'eloquent' as meaning the power to
work in certain ways upon the audience; or if
I say a book is original, and define 'original'
to mean differing from other books, Russell's
logic, if I follow it at all, would seem to doom
me to agreeing that the speech is about elo-
quence, and the book about other books. When
I call a belief true, and define its truth to mean
its workings, I certainly do not mean that the
belief is a belief *about* the workings. It is a
belief about the object, and I who talk about
the workings am a different subject, with a
different universe of discourse, from that of
the believer of whose concrete thinking I profess to give an account.

The social proposition 'other men exist'

and the pragmatist proposition 'it is expedient to believe that other men exist' come from different universes of discourse. One can believe the second without being logically compelled to believe the first; one can believe the first without having ever heard of the second; or one can believe them both. The first expresses the object of a belief, the second tells of one condition of the belief's power to maintain itself. There is no identity of any kind, save the term 'other men' which they contain in common, in the two propositions; and to treat them as mutually substitutable, or to insist that *we* shall do so, is to give up dealing with realities altogether.

Mr. Ralph Hawtrey, who seems also to serve under the banner of abstractionist logic, convicts us pragmatists of absurdity by arguments similar to Mr. Russell's.[1]

As a favor to us and for the sake of the argument, he abandons the word 'true' to our fury, allowing it to mean nothing but the fact

[1] See *The New Quarterly*, for March, 1908.

that certain beliefs are expedient; and he uses the word 'correctness' (as Mr. Pratt uses the word 'trueness') to designate a fact, not about the belief, but about the belief's object, namely that it is as the belief declares it. 'When therefore,' he writes, 'I say it is correct to say that Cæsar is dead, I mean "Cæsar is dead." This must be regarded as the definition of correctness.' And Mr. Hawtrey then goes on to demolish me by the conflict of the definitions. What is 'true' for the pragmatist cannot be what is 'correct,' he says, 'for the definitions are not logically interchangeable; or if we interchange them, we reach the tautology: "Cæsar is dead" means "it is expedient to believe that Cæsar is dead." But what is it expedient to believe? Why, "that Cæsar is dead."' A precious definition indeed of 'Cæsar is dead.'

Mr. Hawtrey's conclusion would seem to be that the pragmatic definition of the truth of a belief in no way implies — what? — that the believer shall believe in his own belief's deliverance? — or that the pragmatist who is talking about him shall believe in that deliverance? The two cases are quite different. For the believer, Cæsar must of course really exist; for the pragmatist critic he need not, for the pragmatic deliverance belongs, as I have just said, to another universe of discourse altogether. When one argues by substituting definition for definition, one needs to stay in the same universe.

The great shifting of universes in this discussion occurs when we carry the word 'truth' from the subjective into the objective realm, applying it sometimes to a property of opinions, sometimes to the facts which the opinions assert. A number of writers, as Mr. Russell himself, Mr. G. E. Moore, and others, favor the unlucky word 'proposition,' which seems expressly invented to foster this confusion, for they speak of truth as a property of 'propositions.' But in naming propositions it is almost impossible not to use the word 'that.' *That* Cæsar is dead, *that* virtue is its own reward, are propositions.

I do not say that for certain logical purposes

it may not be useful to treat propositions as absolute entities, with truth or falsehood inside of them respectively, or to make of a complex like 'that-Cæsar-is-dead' a single term and call it a 'truth.' But the 'that' here has the extremely convenient ambiguity for those who wish to make trouble for us pragmatists, that sometimes it means the *fact* that, and sometimes the *belief* that, Cæsar is no longer living. When I then call the belief true, I am told that the truth means the fact; when I claim the fact also, I am told that my definition has excluded the fact, being a definition only of a certain peculiarity in the belief — so that in the end I have no truth to talk about left in my possession.

The only remedy for this intolerable ambiguity is, it seems to me, to stick to terms consistently. 'Reality,' 'idea' or 'belief,' and the 'truth of the idea or belief,' which are the terms I have consistently held to, seem to be free from all objection.

Whoever takes terms abstracted from all their natural settings, identifies them with definitions, and treats the latter *more algebraico*, not only risks mixing universes, but risks fallacies which the man in the street easily detects. To prove 'by definition' that the statement 'Cæsar exists' is identical with a statement about 'expediency' because the one statement is 'true' and the other is about 'true statements,' is like proving that an omnibus is a boat because both are vehicles. A horse may be defined as a beast that walks on the nails of his middle digits. Whenever we see a horse we see such a beast, just as whenever we believe a 'truth' we believe something expedient. Messrs. Russell and Hawtrey, if they followed their anti-pragmatist logic, would have to say here that we see *that it is* such a beast, a fact which notoriously no one sees who is not a comparative anatomist.

It almost reconciles one to being no logician that one thereby escapes so much abstractionism. Abstractionism of the worst sort dogs Mr. Russell in his own trials to tell positively what the word 'truth' means. In the third of his articles on Meinong, in *Mind*, vol. xiii,

p. 509 (1904), he attempts this feat by limiting the discussion to three terms only, a proposition, its content, and an object, abstracting from the whole context of associated realities in which such terms are found in every case of actual knowing. He puts the terms, thus taken in a vacuum, and made into bare logical entities, through every possible permutation and combination, tortures them on the rack until nothing is left of them, and after all this logical gymnastic, comes out with the following portentous conclusion as what he believes to be 'the correct view: that there is no problem at all in truth and falsehood, that some propositions are true and some false, just as some roses are red and some white, that belief is a certain attitude towards propositions, which is called knowledge when they are true, error when they are false' — and he seems to think that when once this insight is reached the question may be considered closed forever!

In spite of my admiration of Mr. Russell's analytic powers, I wish, after reading such an article, that pragmatism, even had it no other function, might result in making him and other similarly gifted men ashamed of having used such powers in such abstraction from reality. Pragmatism saves us at any rate from such diseased abstractionism as those pages show.

P. S. Since the foregoing rejoinder was written an article on Pragmatism which I believe to be by Mr. Russell has appeared in the *Edinburgh Review* for April, 1909. As far as his discussion of the truth-problem goes, altho he has evidently taken great pains to be fair, it seems to me that he has in no essential respect improved upon his former arguments. I will therefore add nothing further, but simply refer readers who may be curious to pp. 272–280 of the said article.

XV

A DIALOGUE

AFTER correcting the proofs of all that precedes I imagine a residual state of mind on the part of my reader which may still keep him unconvinced, and which it may be my duty to try at least to dispel. I can perhaps be briefer if I put what I have to say in dialogue form. Let then the anti-pragmatist begin : —

Anti-Pragmatist: — You say that the truth of an idea is constituted by its workings. Now suppose a certain state of facts, facts for example of antediluvian planetary history, concerning which the question may be asked : 'Shall the truth about them ever be known ?' And suppose (leaving the hypothesis of an omniscient absolute out of the account) that we assume that the truth is never to be known. I ask you now, brother pragmatist, whether according to you there can be said to be any truth at all about such a state of facts. Is there a truth, or is there not a truth, in cases where at any rate it never comes to be known?

Pragmatist: — Why do you ask me such a question?

Anti-Prag.: — Because I think it puts you in a bad dilemma.

Prag.: — How so?

Anti-Prag.: — Why, because if on the one hand you elect to say that there is a truth, you thereby surrender your whole pragmatist theory. According to that theory, truth requires ideas and workings to constitute it; but in the present instance there is supposed to be no knower, and consequently neither ideas nor workings can exist. What then remains for you to make your truth of?

Prag.: — Do you wish, like so many of my enemies, to force me to make the truth out of the reality itself? I cannot: the truth is something known, thought or said about the reality, and consequently numerically additional to it. But probably your intent is something different; so before I say which horn of your dilemma I choose, I ask you to let me hear what the other horn may be.

Anti-Prag.: — The other horn is this, that if you elect to say that there is *no* truth under the conditions assumed, because there are no ideas or workings, then you fly in the face of common sense. Does n't common sense believe that every state of facts must in the nature of things be truly statable in some kind of a proposition, even tho in point of fact the proposition should never be propounded by a living soul?

Prag.: — Unquestionably common sense believes this, and so do I. There have been innumerable events in the history of our planet of which nobody ever has been or ever will be able to give an account, yet of which it can already be said abstractly that only one sort of possible account can ever be true. The truth about any such event is thus already generically predetermined by the event's nature; and one may accordingly say with a perfectly good conscience that it virtually pre-exists. Common sense is thus right in its instinctive contention.

Anti-Prag.: — Is this then the horn of the dilemma which you stand for? Do you say that there is a truth even in cases where it shall never be known?

Prag.: — Indeed I do, provided you let me hold consistently to my own conception of truth, and do not ask me to abandon it for something which I find impossible to comprehend. — You also believe, do you not, that there is a truth, even in cases where it never shall be known?

Anti-Prag.: — I do indeed believe so.

Prag.: — Pray then inform me in what, according to you, this truth regarding the unknown consists.

Anti-Prag.: — Consists? — pray what do you mean by 'consists'? It consists in nothing but itself, or more properly speaking it has neither consistence nor existence, it obtains, it *holds*.

Prag.: — Well, what relation does it bear to the reality of which it holds?

Anti-Prag.: — How do you mean, 'what relation'? It holds *of* it, of course; it knows it, it represents it.

Prag.: — Who knows it? What represents it?

Anti-Prag.: — The truth does; the truth knows it; or rather not exactly that, but any one knows it who *possesses* the truth. Any true idea of the reality *represents* the truth concerning it.

Prag.: — But I thought that we had agreed that no knower of it, nor any idea representing it was to be supposed.

Anti-Prag.: — Sure enough!

Prag.: — Then I beg you again to tell me in what this truth consists, all by itself, this *tertium quid* intermediate between the facts *per se*, on the one hand, and all knowledge of them, actual or potential, on the other. What is the shape of it in this third estate? Of what stuff, mental, physical, or 'epistemological,' is it built? What metaphysical region of reality does it inhabit?

Anti-Prag.: — What absurd questions! Isn't

it enough to say that it *is true* that the facts are so-and-so, and false that they are otherwise?

Prag.: — 'It' is true that the facts are so-and-so — I won't yield to the temptation of asking you *what* is true; but I do ask you whether your phrase that 'it is true that' the facts are so-and-so really means anything really additional to the bare *being* so-and-so of the facts themselves.

Anti-Prag.: — It seems to mean more than the bare being of the facts. It is a sort of mental equivalent for them, their epistemological function, their value in noetic terms.

Prag.: — A sort of spiritual double or ghost of them, apparently! If so, may I ask you *where* this truth is found.

Anti-Prag.: — Where? where? There is no 'where' — it simply obtains, absolutely obtains.

Prag.: — Not in any one's mind?

Anti-Prag.: — No, for we agreed that no actual knower of the truth should be assumed.

Prag.: — No actual knower, I agree. But are you sure that no notion of a potential or ideal knower has anything to do with forming this strangely elusive idea of the truth of the facts in your mind?

Anti-Prag.: — Of course if there be a truth concerning the facts, that truth is what the ideal knower would know. To that extent you can't keep the notion of it and the notion of him separate. But it is not him first and then it; it is it first and then him, in my opinion.

Prag.: — But you still leave me terribly puzzled as to the status of this so-called truth, hanging as it does between earth and heaven, between reality and knowledge, grounded in the reality, yet numerically additional to it, and at the same time antecedent to any knower's opinion and entirely independent thereof. Is it as independent of the knower as you suppose? It looks to me terribly dubious, as if it might be only another name for a potential as distinguished from an actual knowledge of the reality. Isn't your truth, after all, simply what any successful knower *would* have to know *in case he existed?* And in a universe where no knowers were even conceivable would any truth about the facts there as something numerically distinguishable from the facts themselves, find a place to exist in? To me such truth would not only be non-existent, it would be unimaginable, inconceivable.

Anti-Prag.: — But I thought you said a while ago that there *is* a truth of past events, even tho no one shall ever know it.

Prag.: — Yes, but you must remember that I also stipulated for permission to define the word in my own fashion. The truth of an event, past, present, or future, is for me only another name for the fact that *if* the event ever *does* get known, the nature of the knowledge is already to some degree predetermined. The truth which precedes actual knowledge of a fact means only what any possible knower of the fact will eventually find himself necessitated to believe about it. He must believe something that will bring him into satisfactory relations with it, that will prove a decent mental substitute for it. What this something may be is of course partly fixed already by the nature of the fact and by the sphere of its associations.

This seems to me all that you can clearly mean when you say that truth pre-exists to knowledge. It is knowledge anticipated, knowledge in the form of possibility merely.

Anti-Prag.: — But what does the knowledge know when it comes? Does n't it know the *truth*? And, if so, must n't the truth be distinct from either the fact or the knowledge?

Prag.: — It seems to me that what the knowledge knows is the fact itself, the event, or whatever the reality may be. Where you see three distinct entities in the field, the reality, the knowing, and the truth, I see only two. Moreover, I can see what each of my two entities is *known-as*, but when I ask myself what your third entity, the truth, is known-as, I can find nothing distinct from the reality on the one hand, and the ways in which it may be known on the other. Are you not probably misled by common language, which has found it convenient to introduce a hybrid name, meaning sometimes a kind of knowing and sometimes a reality known, to apply to either of these things interchangeably? And has philosophy anything to gain by perpetuating and consecrating the ambiguity? If you call the object of knowledge 'reality,' and call the manner of its being cognized 'truth,' cognized moreover on particular occasions, and variously, by particular human beings who have their various businesses with it, and if you hold consistently to this nomenclature, it seems to me that you escape all sorts of trouble.

Anti-Prag.: — Do you mean that you think you escape from my dilemma?

Prag.: — Assuredly I escape; for if truth and knowledge are terms correlative and interdependent, as I maintain they are, then wherever knowledge is conceivable truth is conceivable, wherever knowledge is possible truth is possible, wherever knowledge is actual truth is actual. Therefore when you point your first horn at me, I think of truth *actual,* and say it does n't exist. It does n't; for by hypothesis there is no knower, no ideas, no workings. I agree, however, that truth *possible* or *virtual* might exist, for a knower might possibly be brought to birth; and truth *conceivable* certainly exists, for, abstractly taken, there is nothing in the nature of antediluvian events that should make the application of knowledge to them inconceivable. Therefore when you try to impale me on your second horn, I think of the truth in question as a mere abstract possibility, so I say it does exist, and side with common sense.

Do not these distinctions rightly relieve me from embarrassment? And don't you think it might help you to make them yourself?

Anti-Prag.:—Never!—so avaunt with your abominable hair-splitting and sophistry! Truth is truth; and never will I degrade it by identifying it with low pragmatic particulars in the way you propose.

Prag.: — Well, my dear antagonist, I hardly hoped to convert an eminent intellectualist and logician like you; so enjoy, as long as you live, your own ineffable conception. Perhaps the rising generation will grow up more accustomed than you are to that concrete and empirical interpretation of terms in which the pragmatic method consists. Perhaps they may then wonder how so harmless and natural an account of truth as mine could have found such difficulty in entering the minds of men far more intelligent than I can ever hope to become, but wedded by education and tradition to the abstractionist manner of thought.